SHATTERED

*Stories of Lives Broken by Substance Abuse
And How We Put the Pieces Back Together*

by

WHY US KIDS

Shattered: Stories of Lives Broken by Substance Abuse and How We Put the Pieces Back Together

By Why Us Kids

All proceeds will be donated to Why Us Kids nonprofit foundation to help Gracie Parker con-tinue to raise awareness of the youth mental health crisis in our country

1. PSY038000 2. PSY036000 3. SOC072000

Print ISBN: 979-8-9888705-0-0 (paperback)
Ebook ISBN: 979-8-9888705-1-7

Library of Congress Control Number: 2023915011

Otto, North Carolina

Printed in the United States of America

Shattered is a moving collection of short stories that covers the full range of the substance use disorder crisis from the sad final consequences to the joy of recovery, those trying to turn it around, and the call for justice. This is a deeply powerful book that will bring insight and empathy to all who read it."

—DANNY STRONG, American actor, screenwriter, director, producer, and creator of Hulu's miniseries, *Dopesick*, based on Beth Macy's bestselling book, *Dopesick: Dealers, Doctors, and the Drug Company that Addicted America.*

"In *Shattered*, project manager, Casey J., who lost a loved one to drug abuse, examines the impact of substance and alcohol abuse disorders through the lens of those impacted by the disease. In one essay, written by Gracie Parker, a nine-year-old girl, who was raised since infanthood by grandparents and rallies for mental health in her state, we see the fallout that addiction places on families. The reader also hears stories from those who are also making differences in their communities: police, mental health professionals, and those in long-term recovery. These inspired individuals have unpacked their toolkits so that readers may benefit from their wisdom and advice on how to improve the care of the addicted."

—WESLEY C. DAVIDSON, author of the blog, When your Child is Addicted.com, and founder of the Facebook group: Kids on Drugs: Signs, Risks, and How to Get Help!

"*Shattered* does something vital for our time: it turns statistics about trauma, mental health, and addiction issues into real, human stories. All of us surely know someone who has struggled with alcoholism or been swept away by the opioid crisis. And yet we do little more than watch the news and shake our heads, feeling powerless in the face of such monumental struggles. What this book offers are powerful examples of people who are doing more than shake their heads; they're responding as committed artists, devoted therapists, engaged and empathetic law enforcement officers, and passionate activists.

Like *All the Beauty and the Bloodshed*, Laura Poitras's documentary about artist and activist Nan Goldin's battle to expose the Sackler family and the culpability of their company Purdue Pharma, this book reminds us of the power and necessity of art. These survivors, mourning loved ones, and dedicated professionals bring the realities of addiction to light through the book's raw and honest prose. Besides informing and educating us, *Shattered* brings us the deeply engaging stories of people who could have turned inward in the face of such pain, but who have chosen, instead, to speak. Their voices ring out on behalf of those whose suffering we can no longer ignore."

—JOYCE HINNEFELD, author of works of literary fiction including *In Hovering Flight* and *The Beauty of Their Youth*; Emerita Professor of English at Moravian University; and Program Facilitator for Shining Light, an organization dedicated to unlocking the potential in America's prisons.

"By reading *Shattered*, we bear witness to diverse experiences of substance use disorder. It's a prayer-like experience to share in the writers' pains, secrets, and questions. This is more than a collection of stories: it's our history."

—CHARLOTTE BISMUTH, author of *Bad Medicine: Catching New York's Deadliest Pill Pusher*

"The stories in *Shattered* are raw and real. They describe the true nature of addiction from all angles. I've had the pleasure of reading and getting to know these amazing people, and I am so glad their stories are being shared.

Casey is the blood, sweat, and tears of this book, and it started because she went through something traumatic. And then you have nine-year-old Gracie Parker, who lost her mother to drugs at only six months old, and whose father is in and out of jail because of substance abuse. Gracie is using her voice to speak at rallies and started a nonprofit, Why Us Kids, to raise awareness of the youth mental health crisis our country is facing. These brave people chose to share their stories, and they have all inspired me. Addiction is awful and I know from personal experience. But, we can recover and if we do recover out loud, it can reduce the shame and stigma surrounding addiction."

—MICHELE MAIZE, a fellow advocate and friend

TABLE OF
CONTENTS

"When something breaks, if the pieces are large enough, you can fix it. Unfortunately, sometimes things don't break, they shatter. But when you let the light in, shattered glass will glitter. And in those moments when the pieces of what we were catch the sun, I'll remember just how beautiful it was."

Jenny Young from the movie *Someone Great*

In Loving Memory

of

Eddie Bisch—1982–2001

JTH—1971–2011

WCM—1978–2013

Anna Jane Moseley—1990–2013

Cody Souders—1995–2013

Jade Stark—1983–2015

Ben Miller—1992–2016

REM—1986–2021

FOREWORD

E VERYONE READING THIS book has someone—a friend, a relative, or a close family member—who struggles with addiction. In the twenty years I have served as a mental health therapist and addiction counselor, I have had a front-row seat to the ugly face of addiction. I have seen the destructive path substance abuse has taken in the lives of many of my clients, friends, and even family.

In 2011, I started a nonprofit addiction recovery support program called Addict II Athlete (AIIA). AIIA uses health, sports, and recreation to erase addiction by replacing it with something of more positive value, such as healthy recreation, team unity, relationships, sportsmanship, and accountability. I became a coach and used my therapeutic background to lay the foundations of recovery by no longer being anonymous.

We decided that the old mindset of anonymity was no longer appropriate for this new generation that is battling such severe addictions. By keeping our stories confined to ourselves, we cannot help others who struggle. I began to understand the truth behind addiction and how challenging it can be for an individual to overcome it without having the right tools, environment, and most importantly, people behind them.

Early in my career, I heard about the rule of thirds. One-third of everyone who struggles with addiction will somehow find a way out of it and not stumble again. Unfortunately, the next third of those who struggle with addiction will be in and out of incarceration and rehabilitation centers. They will struggle with symptoms of addiction for the rest of their lives. Unfortunately, the last third will succumb to the addiction and pass away, whether by overdose, accident or directly linked to the addiction itself.

The rule of thirds was very challenging for me to conceptualize. It meant that two-thirds of those struggling with addiction suffer a significant loss. *But be aware that those who have passed away from the disease gave you, the reader, a gift—that you may continue to be part of the third that will make it.* Learn their stories, and share them with those who struggle, so that gift may ultimately lead you or your loved one to recovery and healing.

We have all been waiting for "them" to come and save us from this epidemic. We have waited for the police, the doctors, the government, and the troops to rescue us. The simple truth is, the troops aren't coming, dear reader; you are the troops.

We can no longer wait for someone else to do it for us. The time is now, and we need to step up and take the leadership position to become actively engaged in our community and homes to ensure the stories you read in this book are not ignored or forgotten.

Thank you for reading this book. I know it is not easy to go through a loss, especially a painful and traumatic one. I also know that you may have been told by others or even yourself that you can do nothing about it, but that's not true. You are still here, and so are others you love. You will never be alone in your grief because we are all connected in this world by our humanity, and there's no shame in sharing your story with others who have gone through similar experiences.

This book can help others heal from losing a loved one due to addiction, overdose, or other adverse effects of substance abuse. I hope that it gives them some comfort knowing they're not alone in their grief and maybe even offers them some guidance on moving forward from their pain to heal themselves so they can also begin healing others. It's up to us to turn this mess into a powerful message.

Coach Blu Robinson, CMHC, SUDC
Head Coach of Addict II Athlete
Clinical Mental Health Therapist, Substance Use Disorder Counselor

https://www.addicttoathlete.com/

Blu Robinson, founder of Addict II Athlete (photo credit: Blu Robinson)

INTRODUCTION

WHEN YOU THINK of substance use disorder, what is the first thought that comes to mind? A disease of the brain? Or a conscious choice to use due to a character flaw? Some will argue it is a treatable mental illness, others will say that the substance abuser can stop but doesn't want to. Is it possible that the answer lies somewhere in the middle? Why is it that some people fight their inner demons while others feed them? (If you've never read the Cherokee tale of the two wolves, please do.)

People *have* recovered. They fight the urge to use every day. People can do it—if they really want to. Unfortunately, many end up losing their battle. These people are mothers, fathers, sisters, brothers, sons, daughters, cousins, and friends. These people's lives had meaning, and their deaths will not be in vain. Their lives inspired us to take action, thus creating our group, Healing Lotus Hearts—rising from the darkest of times and sharing a message of hope and love.

Healing Lotus Hearts first came together in early 2023. We're from different backgrounds and we met in different ways, but we share similar stories, allowing us to understand and support one another. Above all, we share a common goal—to help others and break the stigma around substance abuse.

It was during this time, activist, Ed Bisch, was kind enough to connect us with Miss Gracie Parker, founder of Why Us Kids nonprofit organization. She was brave enough to share her tragic story with us and her future goals. We have so much faith in her mission, and we believe she will fight as hard as she humanly can for youth mental health. We need someone like her to speak up for those who cannot, and we hope all of our stories will encourage readers to share theirs.

Shattered is a compilation of personal essays told by authors who have experienced addiction in various ways and based on our memories of specific events. Several authors lost loved ones to overdoses or alcoholism;

some recovered and sought to help others on the path to recovery. Some of our authors witnessed the effects of substance use disorder firsthand through their professions or within their circle of family and friends. Our stories offer multiple perspectives so readers can see the effects of addiction on the whole community, not just the user.

We want you to feel our sadness, our anger, and our frustration, but also our strength and our healing. We want you to know that it's okay to feel vulnerable. There are so many people struggling; you are not alone. We are all on our own journeys, and we are all works in progress. We hope that after reading our stories you will realize that even though addiction is powerful, your will to live is even stronger.

We want people to understand that addiction doesn't care what race, ethnicity, sex, class, or age you are. It doesn't discriminate. Once the disease sinks its talons into you, it re-wires your brain. You may feel trapped as if there is no way out of the hell that has consumed you. But there is hope. Addiction can be treated. Some treatments may work better than others, and some may not work at all, but that doesn't mean you should give up. It just means you find a different avenue until you discover one that works for you. It won't be easy, but nothing worth doing ever is.

If you need help, please seek professional treatment (we included several resources at the back of our book).

Trigger Warning: Chapters one through five, fourteen, sixteen, and seventeen discuss the death of a loved one. If you have experienced a recent loss, these may be difficult chapters for you to read.

With love,
Healing Lotus Hearts & Why Us Kids

"Find the seed at the bottom of your heart and bring forth a flower."

Shigenori Kameoka

PART ONE

THE RIPPLE EFFECT

"Addiction begins with the hope that something "out there" can instantly fill up the emptiness inside."

Jean Kilbourne

CHAPTER ONE

DEATH IS THE DOORWAY

By Hannah Souders

DEATH IS A big scary word, ain't it? It's the thing we rarely talk about, the thing we're all heading toward, the thing that shocks our worlds and shapes us into who we actually are. We are granted gifts in the face of death that are not found anywhere else. There is profound learning done in the shadows of excruciating pain; the type you'd never quite grasp until you've found yourself lying among the ashes of what was. And you look around, while you sink lower into the depths of your pain than you'd ever thought was possible, and you see clearly for the first time. In these moments, you learn what truly matters. Layers of yourself you've never met, feelings you didn't think existed, and the emergence of something larger than yourself.

When life decides to give you death, you are shifted into deep questioning, longing, and seeking. And when you face the Creator for the first time, it's usually in the face of Destruction. You are naked; stripped of all you thought was true. And from this place, you can see (beyond all your previous understandings) the walls inside which you've comfortably existed. While you watch the rest of the world continue to spin, your corner of it stands completely still. In these moments of wild vulnerability, you are witnessing all your pain, not the pain itself. And that presence will never leave you, its only job is to offer the tender love of awareness.

In granting yourself permission to feel the ugliest of emotions, you grant yourself permission to feel the most beautiful aspects of this human experience. For as deep as your grief has traveled, your capacity to see and be *love* equally grows. The gift is in the exploration: diving back into the abyss, over and over again, question after question, with no wants other than to learn. It usually doesn't make sense until it does. So stay the course and feel the discomfort, with full trust in your heart that it is the exact thing your soul needs to heal.

If I've learned anything from my 18-year-old brother's death, it is that humans are intensely afraid of the things we don't understand. It's much easier to make assumptions about others than to dive into the murky waters that occupy the underworld of addiction and death. But why? What are we afraid of? Of getting stuck there too? We are all equally likely to get sucked into the abyss, and we all will arrive when it is our time. The thing that matters is how you transform this place, how you face it, and how you stand up again, wiser. This life is arduous, relentless, and undeniably beautiful. There is no escaping the ebb and flow of its grandeur.

The memory of my mother's shrill scream the morning we found him still straightens my spine. A new reality was born when I was thirteen years old. One that consisted of blurred vision, confusion, and wild discovery. I sat in the ICU, watching *Law and Order*, surely hoping the solving of heinous crimes would provide a subconscious resolution to the destruction of the life I used to know. I sat completely still as my eyes followed each nurse who entered the room, just another patient, just another bag to refill.

I had never experienced a moment like that. Where I could see the entire Earth continue to rotate on its axis while my world had completely fallen off its perfect tilt and was plummeting into the deep dark underworld of unfamiliarity. I watched as hundreds of old friends, family members, acquaintances, and even enemies walked into the hospital to visit my brother as he lay unconscious with tubes falling from his face. These moments taught me more about vulnerability than any other. To open the doors and allow others to bear witness to the crumbling of our reality was painstakingly freeing. We slept on the floor of the waiting room for five nights. I couldn't tell you what was spoken within those four walls. It was a blur of dissociation, courage, fear, rage, and a love I had never tasted before.

To be in this liminal space, so very close to destruction, at the end of someone's life, on the bridge back to full emergence with the Divine, is something impossible to understand until you've faced it yourself. I held his ice-cold, fluid-filled hand for hours as tears dug holes into my prepubescent skin. Knowing a moment would come that would be the last. I clung to each second I had left as my heart ached with each beat.

He lives on in various bodies; bodies that have continued to wander the Earth, wherever their hearts ask them to go. I always wonder if they felt any part of them shift once they took on a piece of my brother's being. Maybe his heart lent a passion for slimy geckos, or his skin a layer of protection and grit for a vulnerable soul, his liver a renewed sense of adventure, his eyes a new perspective on life.

Pain is a great doorway. Maybe the most powerful of them all. It challenges your belief systems and makes you tune into what is real and what is true. What actually matters to your heart. Where you can shed all the rest. It makes you honest. It makes you tired and cold. But it also lights up your system in a way that shows you that you are alive. You are alive in your fumbling about. You are alive in your squirming. You are alive in the dying. We are in constant cycles of life and death, as we feel versions of ourselves die off as our souls gain wisdom and outgrow their old shells. Change and impermanence are some of the only absolutes we have. Can we lean on these truths? Can we use them to find greater awareness and appreciation for the moments of reprieve?

Healing comes in the release of our grip. It comes in the moments we give ourselves full permission to feel our feelings, act like wild animals, scream at the top of our lungs, and voice our frustrations with the Universe and its unfair rhythms. There is great purification in the allowance of our fullness.

I am in debt to my brother and the transformation his passing brought to my life. It's a strange thing to say, that one of the most detrimental events in my story was also the key to my liberation. It seems this is the case for all forms of life/death cycles, whether you are saying goodbye to a loved one's soul or goodbye to a version of you that you never thought you'd outgrow. It is all excruciating. But the pain carves a map that you will follow to find your deepest truths. It shows you the way out, the way to others, the way to life. We are constantly changing, shedding, and killing off pieces of ourselves that no longer equate to who we are becoming. Make room for the lessons offered through your suffering. The mind sees death as an ending, while the soul knows death as an awakening to a new world.

Most of all, I want you to know that I love you. I love your pain. I love your confusion. I am standing with you as you navigate the treacherous landscapes of your heart and mind. There are infinite others who also meet you in this foreign space. I'm with you as you ache, as you question what the point is of all this, when you want to call it quits, and when the waves of emotion feel too intense for one human body to comprehend. Lean on me, lean on us, lean on yourself. Know there is extraordinary beauty waiting for you on the other side. I promise you your anguish will grant you unimaginable experiences. It will break you free from worlds that don't serve you and throw you into anomalous lands that will cause growth and expansion in ways you never would have chosen.

Hannah was in awe of her big brother's fine catch. (photo credit: Hannah Souders, 2002)

"Though no one can go back and make a brand new start, anyone can start from now and make a brand new ending."

Carl Bard

CHAPTER TWO

FIGHTING A LOSING BATTLE

By Casey J.

Don't do drugs. I wrote that line imagining Coach Carr from *Mean Girls* saying it. "Don't do drugs because you will overdose and die. Just don't do them, promise?"

I'll admit to experimenting with a few different substances in my younger years (late teens to mid-twenties). I think it's become normal for people to want to try drugs for fun—to escape the real world, to relieve stress, to cope, to rebel, to feel something different (or to feel nothing at all). I smoked pot during my senior year of high school to fit in; I didn't want to be a bigger loser than I already thought I was. I wanted to be liked. I wanted to belong. Pot made me "cool." (This is the part where you roll your eyes and sigh.)

But once you stray away from marijuana, you enter into a whole new realm of drugs (in my opinion). My experimental phase was very short-lived (and by that, I mean two times and done). I didn't like not being in control of what I was doing. I didn't like feeling paranoid, uneasy, and physically ill. My body couldn't handle the toxins. Not my idea of fun by any means. A couple of bad experiences are all that it took—I didn't want to dabble anymore with anything. I was scared. But then there are people at the opposite end of the spectrum who love being high and crave their next fix.

I will never fully understand addiction, because I don't suffer from it, and hope I never do. But I know firsthand what it can do in a relationship—it will suck the life force out of you and destroy any possibility of true happiness. Addiction is a beast. I empathize with those who struggle with their active substance use disorder or their sobriety. I saw how addiction consumed my boyfriend. It sunk its claws into him and refused to let go. It wanted him dead. And it won.

So, here I am, sharing my story in memory of the man who whisked me away on the wildest ride of my life, and in the process, gave me a beautiful son.

Riley was handsome, charismatic, intelligent, funny (his witty sense of humor was spot on), and talented. Boy, was he talented. That man could create anything out of a piece of wood. His woodworking skills were truly admirable. He started a successful business and was finally doing what he loved. I was so proud of him and in awe of his gift.

But he also had a dark side. He suffered from depression, anxiety, and above all, substance use disorder. The drugs filled any internal voids and made him feel like he was floating on a cloud. I was a fool to think I could compete with that. I couldn't offer him what his addiction needed. It was exhausting trying to figure out which side of him I was going to deal with on any given day.

Dating him was like dating two people. There was Riley and then there was his demon. Riley was a beautiful, kind, fun, loving soul. He was a good person with a big heart. Once the drugs took hold, Riley stepped out of the spotlight and into the shadows. The "dark shit" transformed him into someone I didn't even recognize. His once bright, smiling face appeared drawn out. His skin would change from olive-colored to a ghostly white; his glassy, soulless eyes sported pinned pupils, which usually rolled up into their sockets; and drool would dribble out of his gaping mouth. Riley was gone, and this thing—this demon—ran the show. I tried to help him, but I was no match. I was fighting a losing battle from day one.

When we first met in 2017, I immediately fell for his charm—his contagious smile and laugh, his curly dark brown hair, and his friendly brown eyes. It was hard to believe he swiped right for me.

We hit it off on our first date at a local restaurant and planned a hike for our second date. We met at a nearby state park, and I brought my beloved retriever, Rosie, to meet him. Her reaction would make or break his potential as relationship material. I remember she jumped out of the car and ran over to his wide-open arms. She licked his trimmed beard and wagged not just her tail, but her whole butt! She must have mistaken his facial hair for dog fur. They were instantly two peas in a pod. He loved her and she loved him. There was no turning back.

Riley had this way of making me feel alive. He lived his life by his rules, and nobody could tell him otherwise. He was wild and free. A part of me envied him for this (to an extent). I was usually more uptight and worried a lot about everything under the sun—things I could control and things I couldn't. I wanted to be more carefree. He was a breath of fresh air, and I loved breathing in his musk.

Our fondness for each other grew, and eventually, we took the relationship to the next level. The sex was mind-blowing. I remember thinking that it was too good to be true. And it was. (Food for thought: sex has a way of clouding your judgment. I later realized our sex was what I desired in the relationship. It made me feel loved and wanted. I craved that deep, meaningful connection. The unfortunate truth is that while I longed for intimacy with him, he longed for drugs.)

The day after our first time, I saw him in a state I wish I hadn't. I drove to his house to hang out, and as soon as I parked in the driveway, he stumbled through the front door and toward me. His face was pale, he could barely stand upright, and he kept nodding off. I didn't know what was going on. *Was he drunk? High on muscle relaxers?* Simultaneously, I felt an instant sadness in my heart for him, and an overwhelming wave of anxiety crashed over me. *He needs help. Maybe you can help him. No. Run away. Don't look back, just run far away.*

He convinced me to stay. He swore it would never happen again but that his shoulder was in a great deal of pain, and he needed to take something to feel better. (Years before, he was in a bad car accident. He was prescribed oxy, and well, the rest is history.) My gut told me to cut him off, but my heart wanted to believe it was a mistake that he wouldn't repeat.

First lesson learned: when your gut tells you to get the fuck out of there, you listen to it, and get the fuck out of there.

The second lesson learned: no matter how hard you try, you can't change anybody. Please remember that. It will save you a ton of heartache. You are your own responsibility. Take care of yourself first or else you will lose yourself in the process of loving someone who despises their very existence. Sometimes, there are external forces that are too powerful to overcome. Sometimes, love doesn't conquer all.

I believed if I loved him, if I cared for him, and supported him, he would find the motivation to seek professional treatment. He didn't think he had a problem so why bother? I forced him to talk to two different therapists: one he easily manipulated, and the other he claimed made fun of him during their first and only session. He attended NA meetings here and there, but he either went high or got high right after they ended. He was only going through the motions for me; he wasn't ready to commit. He didn't want to enroll in detox programs or in/outpatient rehab facilities, because he believed they didn't work. He didn't want to try Suboxone. He didn't want to try, and I didn't know what else to do.

I don't know if he thought the road to recovery was too intimidating, and he was afraid to put in the work or afraid of failing and appearing weak, or fearful of having to relive any buried childhood trauma. I don't know what was going through his head because he rarely opened up about it. He kept everything bottled up and numbed his pain with drugs and alcohol. He was a prisoner in his mind. The drugs acted as temporary solutions for permanent problems. He needed to dig deep and unearth the root cause, but he refused to venture down that path. Nothing I said or did for him changed his mind. It was like talking to a brick wall. I was intentionally drowning myself while attempting to keep him afloat.

Our relationship unraveled, but I fought to stay. I made excuse after excuse. *Am I capable of saving him? Will he change for me? What am I trying to prove? He doesn't even care about himself, so why should I? Because you love him and don't want anything bad to happen to him. Because if you abandon him and he overdoses and dies, you will feel guilty. You will feel responsible for it. Don't give up on him. He needs you and you need him.* He wasn't my responsibility, but I made it my job to try to protect him from the evil surrounding him. I was committed to him—to saving him.

We went 'round and 'round in circles—the same arguments followed by denials by both of us. The more I tried to help or, in his eyes, control him, the harder he pushed back. In August 2018, I found the courage to initiate a break. I still loved and cared for him, so I had a very hard time cutting off contact. It should have been a clean break, but relationships are messy, and humans, well, are human. I hoped he would wake up and realize what he was losing. I wanted him to value me, but truth be told, I didn't even value myself. During our break, we continued having sex. I wasn't ready to let go. Was it a wise decision? Absolutely not, but I don't regret it one bit.

I ended up in the ER due to a ruptured ovarian cyst, and lo and behold, I learned I was pregnant. I think I saw his eyes pop out of his skull, fall onto the floor, and roll out of the room. *Will having a baby save him?* A word of advice—bringing a baby into this world isn't going to change a damn thing (and that applies to any shitty situation). If anything, it sent him spiraling downward at the speed of light.

The next nine months were a nightmare. He couldn't cope with the fact that he was going to be a father. He didn't want his son to think he was a fuck up, so he used drugs to make those thoughts go away. He refused to remove any of his known triggers and enablers, despite knowing deep down he needed a clean slate.

He moved in with my parents and me to curb his drug use in the winter of 2019. During this time, he managed to land a full-time job at a reputable company. He continued using. His addiction infected my whole family. I felt guilty for bringing it into their lives. I hoped every day that he would find the strength to get better. At one point, I just hoped he would live to see the birth of his son.

A few months later, our son, Ty, was born, and Riley was right by my side during labor. He was great. I was impressed with how well he did. I remember staring at Riley holding Ty like a football. Ty was wrapped up like a little burrito while Riley gazed down at his sleeping face. It was a beautiful moment, and I knew Riley would be an amazing dad. I couldn't wait for our little family to flourish.

By the time Ty was a month old, he had already ventured out on three separate hikes. We loved enjoying the warm weather and listening to the sounds nature had to offer. In September 2019, Riley reserved a camping spot for us in Shenandoah National Park. We hiked cool paths. Riley cooked us delicious meals while Ty, Rosie, and I sat around the fire and listened to music.

In March 2020, we rented a place of our own. It was exciting—things were finally looking up for us. Riley was doing great. In the fall of 2020, we embarked on our journey north to Bar Harbor, Maine to visit Acadia National Park for a week. In the summer of 2021, we explored Lake George and Lake Placid in upstate New York for an extended weekend. And then we drove to West Virginia to visit my younger sister. Little did I know that would be our last family vacation.

The months leading up to Riley's untimely death were like a ticking time bomb. His drug use kicked into high gear in the winter and spring of 2021, so Ty, Rosie, and I spent more time living at my parents' house. His physical features began to change. He appeared more tired and run down. He wasn't eating as much food, so he was losing weight. I can't tell you how many candy wrappers I found scattered throughout his car (this coming from a person who didn't even like candy and desserts—that's a slight lie, he loved Friendly's strawberry milkshakes). I remember telling him one day in my parents' garage, while he was building a beautiful dining room river table, that I thought he was sick; that I thought he was dying. I was watching him slowly die, and I didn't even fully realize it at the time.

We argued constantly. I couldn't understand why he wasn't trying harder for his son. And he couldn't understand why I kept "taking his son away from him." I was angry, frustrated, and heartbroken. I know I said so many mean things. I called him a coward, selfish, pathetic, weak, and worse. I wish I could take the insults back, but I was ignorant and didn't understand. Fear got the best of me and I lashed out. I took it personally when I shouldn't have. I wanted him to be the dad I knew he could be. I wanted him to be my partner. I wanted my family together but his addiction was tearing us apart.

His addiction hit me like a train on Monday, July 19, 2021. Ty, Rosie, and I went back to the apartment that evening for dinner and found Riley unconscious on his work table in the spare room. I remember shaking his shoulder when all of a sudden, he shot up like a bat out of hell and fell to the floor with a thud. His arms were sticking up in the air, slightly bent; his clammy skin was grayish-yellow, and I could only see the whites in his eyes. Thinking he was playing, Rosie jumped on top of him and licked his beard while wagging her tail. (Bless her little heart.) While holding Ty, I bent down, pushed Rosie off of him, and smacked him in the face—screaming at him to wake up. Ty started crying. I called 911. Riley came to and crawled out of the workroom. He stared at me in shock, humiliation, and disappointment. I think it killed him knowing his son saw him in that condition.

The ambulance brought Riley to the hospital despite his refusing to go. All he kept saying was "I wasn't trying to hurt anybody. Why can't I hear anything?" Even once he was at the hospital, he STILL refused to admit it was an overdose. When I visited him in the hospital, the doctor showed me his drug screen, and he only tested positive for marijuana. They didn't test him for fentanyl. Why? I don't know. And I didn't even think to ask at the time. I was just glad he was alive. I still had Riley here with me, and that was all that mattered. I hoped the incident would be an eye-opener to get help, but it wasn't.

That overdose was a death sentence. Riley was broken. I had seen him depressed before, but not like that. He was a shell of a man. I begged him not to get lost in his head; not to let his demons get the best of him. I drilled it into his head that we wouldn't abandon him; we would stay and support him, but he needed help. On a subconscious level, I knew he wasn't strong enough to crawl out of his dark abyss, but I hoped. I hoped he would for his son. I loved him, and I needed him here with me. Exactly one week later, he decided to use again, and I didn't make it home in time to save him.

I remember looking at the clock around 1:30 in the afternoon and thinking that I hadn't heard from Riley in a while. I called him, but he didn't answer. I began to worry and made numerous calls and texts over the next couple of hours—still no answer. I knew he was dead.

I raced back to our apartment from my parents' house. I talked to myself in the car—attempting to prepare myself to find him dead. But nothing can prepare you for finding someone dead, let alone the person you love. I sped down our narrow, windy street, and as soon as I entered our driveway, I spotted his SUV sitting at the top of the hill. My heart sank.

I fumbled to get my key into the front door and unlock it. The apartment was cold and silent. I ran up the carpeted steps. The thuds beneath my anxious feet were deafening. I rounded the corner and saw him face down on the cream-colored sectional couch. I yelled his name, "Riley! Riley!" And hurried toward him. I stopped in my tracks and scanned his lifeless body. His face was smothered in his arm and blanket, and his legs were covered in purple splotches. His feet were dark purple. I touched his left shoulder, and it was cold. I kneeled and lifted his head. The center of his face was blue. His mouth hung open. One eyelid was closed while the other remained open. He was dead. I thought I was going to faint. I wanted him to wake up. I called 911 and ran next door to alert our landlords.

I returned to our apartment, and sat next to Riley, holding his cold, lifeless hand. I cried. *This can't be real. He's going to wake up. You're going to wake up. This is a nightmare, and he's going to be okay. Riley promised we would move out west and start fresh. He promised he would teach Ty how to snowboard, rock climb, camp, and work with wood. He promised to join Boys Scouts with him. This can't be happening. Please, wake up.* Except I wasn't dreaming, and he wasn't going to wake up. In the blink of an eye, my worst fears had come true. He was gone, and I was going to be raising our two-year-old son without him. All our hopes and dreams were shattered over fucking drugs.

Riley was thirty-four when fentanyl ended his life. Thirty-four years old. Just let that sink in for a bit. He didn't deserve it. But life isn't fair; it was never meant to be. I lost my boyfriend, the father of my son, and my best friend that fateful day. I will never be the same person I was. It's overwhelming at times learning to navigate this new chapter without him. I think of him and grieve him every single day. I grieve the future we should have had together. I grieve the fact that drugs robbed Ty of growing up with an awesome dad.

Throughout all of this, I learned you can't change the past, but you can accept it in order to move forward. He would want us to live and enjoy life. He would want us to embark on fun-filled adventures and create new memories. I know he's with us because I can feel his presence every now and then. Sometimes he even visits me in my dreams to hang out with us. They are beautiful moments, for we are a whole family once again.

"People spend a lifetime searching for happiness, looking for peace. They chase idle dreams, addictions, religions, and even other people, hoping to fill the emptiness that plagues them. The irony is the only place they ever needed to search was within."

Ramona L. Anderson

CHAPTER THREE

SOMETIMES THE ONLY PERSON YOU CAN SAVE IS YOURSELF

By Nanci Hummer

MY DIVORCE BECAME final in 2005, and I was moving myself and four kids to a new town, new state, and new chapter. I wanted to believe that divorcing their father and moving away from the place that I/we called home was going to change everything in my life, including myself...and boy did it! Once we were settled into our new home, new routine, and new normal, I found myself in a new way of earning quick cash and that was bartending. I enjoyed meeting new people and in some odd way, it made me feel important, as I wasn't aware of how to do that for myself. After a few bartending jobs, I found myself at yet a new bartending gig and knew that this was the place where I was going to find my person, my love, and my happiness.

In May of 2007, I did just that, but it truly wasn't the path I intended to travel to get there. As I was getting ready to leave my shift one night, there was one table that had yet to close out its tab. A table of off-duty, local policemen with one empty chair. I asked where their invisible friend was, and they stated that he was in his vehicle on the phone. I made a few jokes, wondering if he needed a trail of beer to find his way or if I needed to take it to the car. Eventually, he made his way in, and I asked if they needed anything else before I left, and one of his friends stated, "Yes, your number for him." I quickly responded with, "Okay, as long as he's going to use it." And that was how it all began.

Our first date consisted of going to a local restaurant/bar to grab something to eat. We never did eat that night, though. Every time food was brought up, he would say, "In a little while." We were so caught up in the magic that was transpiring between us that before I knew it, a little while never came. Did I believe it was odd? Yes, but we all know how first dates can go sometimes. Or did I just want to disregard that we didn't eat, but that he did do quite a bit of drinking that night?

I found out that he had served our country in the army. He loved the camaraderie of a platoon, which was the reason that he went through the police academy. Eventually, he became a K-9 officer, and he was a really good one. He had a German shepherd, and that dog loved the fool out of him. He also shared with me that his father had passed from a heart attack, and he recently moved back to the township where he grew up to be closer to his mom. All of these things, and more, that he shared with me put me in total awe of him and the hope of where this could go. I had such high hopes.

We stayed in touch, went on a few more dates, and before you knew it, I was introducing him to my kids. I was falling in love. One moment that sticks out to me was an afternoon when I was at his home, and he asked me to grab the vodka out of the freezer. I had never seen that done before (even as a bartender) and thought that was a great idea...only to find out later that by storing it in the freezer, it didn't need to be diluted with ice when making a drink.

We dated on and off for over five years. He was a part of my children's lives and a part of my extended family. I believed I was a part of his. I was in a situation where my children were on the younger side, and I didn't have the luxury of dropping everything that I was doing to go and see him or do things, which led to him spending quite a bit of time at my home and having some day dates. I was able to have date nights every other weekend, which always involved drinking. I wasn't a huge drinker but liked to have a few drinks to unwind on the weekends. We went to the movies one night and he bought me a bottle of wine—three actually. I tried hard to keep up with him; he brought the alcohol into the movie theater with us. The movie that was on the big screen was *The Hangover*, but I have never seen it, as I ended up in the ladies' room for most of it getting sick.

I knew deep down in my heart that the more time I spent with him, the more the red flags of alcoholism were slapping me in the face. I would bring things up to him that were bothering me, but they always managed to get twisted back to me. I knew that he was a good guy, but just had a problem with alcohol. You may be asking yourself, if I was seeing these red flags, why did I stay? I stayed because I loved him more than I loved myself. I didn't believe that anyone else would want me and stayed because I didn't have enough faith in myself to know that I needed to love myself. I dragged my children into situations I am embarrassed about when I look back, but always managed to find an excuse to stay. I take full responsibility for the part that I played in this relationship. I became addicted to the highs and lows of it all. I knew that the lack of trust I had in him and the relationship was not helping at all. The insecurities grew, and the fighting grew even more.

I begged him to quit drinking—let's have a weekend or a night with no alcohol. I wouldn't drink but would smell it on his breath. He worked the night shift, and I always enjoyed the mornings he texted me inviting me for breakfast after the kids got on the bus, because I knew he was as sober as he was going to be for the day if he wasn't working, and we could have a clear-headed conversation. Many times we did...it truly was my favorite time of day with him. Sometimes, he would pay his bills by writing out checks, and his hands would shake terribly. I would ask him what was wrong, and he would respond with "They shake because I'm super tired." Was I extremely naive during this time of my life as I wanted to believe that when a person spoke, they were stating the truth? Maybe, but boy, did I learn.

You may be asking what I loved about him. I loved his smile. He was fun and spontaneous. I loved that he was twelve years younger than me, and it didn't seem to matter to him. He always said that age was only a number. I felt that he loved me for me. He saw things in me that I was unable to see in myself. The sex was amazing. I loved the fact that he had a solid job. I loved the way he enjoyed spending quality time with my kids. He taught me how to have fun, not just with him, but with my kids as well.

I loved the moments when I felt safe. He was such an amazing hugger. Best hugs! He had one of the biggest hearts of anyone I had ever met. I loved the hope of the dream that I believed we could be. He was an extremely powerful human. Not just physically, but emotionally too. He had such charisma...beautiful eyelashes and a smile that would make you stop in your tracks. As far as I was concerned, he was my forever, and he always stated that I was his. Realistically though, our relationship was extremely toxic. I was just as addicted to him as he was addicted to alcohol.

In 2010, he knew that alcohol was destroying him—destroying us. He tried to quit cold turkey, but at this point, he was drinking a handle of vodka a day and to quit the way that he did quite often, is deadly. We were both at work when I received a phone call that he was being taken to the hospital as he was having a seizure. I froze. I couldn't bring myself to go to the hospital right away, and finally, a coworker told me that I needed to go. I ended up taking my daughter with me and we went to the emergency room. I witnessed him having another seizure, and I lost it. I had never witnessed one before, and I truly didn't know what to do. Once that passed, the nurse began asking him questions. He was not being truthful, and she looked to me for the answers—for the honesty that would help him. I would nod my head with the real answer hoping that he wouldn't see me doing it.

He was in the hospital for three days. They ran all types of tests. I was put in touch with an addictions counselor at the hospital for him, and I begged her for some answers. I will never forget asking her what I needed to do to help him, and she looked at me like a deer in headlights and responded with "I don't know." I felt so helpless. The doctor had asked to talk to me and stated that my boyfriend's liver enzyme level was 3,000 times higher than it was supposed to be and that if he didn't quit drinking, he would be dead within three years. That was a huge responsibility to put on me, but I was going to do what I could to help him. I loved him. I was invested. I was desperate.

I contacted some of his friends, but I was unable to facilitate an intervention. Perhaps they didn't want to get involved, perhaps they looked at me as the crazy girlfriend, perhaps they were as lost as I was and just didn't know what to do. I will never know their reasons but respect the decisions that they made as they were all on their own journey. This was mine. This was his. This was ours. He came home from the hospital and life as he knew it went back to "normal." No follow-up doctor appointments, and no AA meetings at this point. He was drinking but not in front of me anymore.

I put myself and my children in extremely dangerous situations. We decided to go to an amusement park. He met us at my home, and we left from there. It was early in the morning, and he had just gotten off of work and wanted to drive. Considering the time of day, I felt it was fine. My four kids, my daughter's boyfriend, and I all hopped in the car, and we were ready to go. As we began to enter the ramp leading to the highway, there was a yield sign along with a tractor-trailer going over the speed limit in the right-hand lane. My boyfriend didn't yield. He didn't even slow down. I yelled that he needed to yield, and he yelled back that the truck needed to yield. By the grace of God, we were spared, and I yelled at him to pull over for about the next four miles. Eventually, he did, and as we both walked behind the car, he said to me that I was an embarrassment and I responded with, "No, you are the embarrassment." At that moment, I began to take my power back...if I couldn't do it for myself, those four lives that called me mom needed me to stop this!

As we made our way into the amusement park, the younger kids dragged us to the first ride. My daughter and I decided to sit this one out, and she looked at me and said, "Either you go through his backpack or I will." Of course, I did, and in there was a full Gatorade bottle of vodka. I dumped it out without his knowledge and went about the rest of the day. No one spoke about what was found and what was now missing from his backpack. As we hopped on rides, I made a point of sitting next to him...an alcoholic with no alcohol on a ride that states seizure warnings. Good times, said no one ever!

I continued to distance myself a little bit more, but somehow always managed to find my way back. Both of his parents had passed away before he had turned 30, and my heart just ached for him. I wanted to be there. I wanted to be his family. He referred to the kids and me as such and I believed that family never deserted family. I just didn't know what was best at this point. I would pull away and then go back. There were a lot of fights. Cheating. A lot of physical abuse. We were both so broken. I believed the only glue that I had was him. The longest amount of time I distanced myself at this point was three months. I began dating someone else and again, always found my way back with the hope that this time was going to be different. He was my drug. I was addicted to saving him.

He finally decided to go to rehab. I was so grateful. After numerous phone calls, we finally found a facility that would take his insurance. What a debacle, but ultimately, we did what we needed to do to get him the help he was finally ready to receive. The ride there was so scary. I got lost, and he was getting so sick, I was so afraid he would have a seizure. Once we arrived, the check-in began. They made a point of telling him that dating me was a huge mistake because I was a bartender. I really didn't understand that at the time, but I was still willing to do whatever it took to help him. I drove home that day breathing a sigh of relief. He/we were finally on the road to recovery. I went through his home while he was there to remove any alcohol that was hidden. His brother and I found eleven bottles of vodka. The situation was even worse than I had imagined, and it broke my heart.

After two weeks, his brother and I drove down to see him. On the way, he asked me, "Why are you here? I don't have a choice, but you do. You can leave." I responded with, "I love him."

We were able to see him that day after attending a family meeting. I was so excited, I believed that this was the chance that I had been waiting for. When I saw him, he took my breath away. He looked and felt so healthy. I decided that I was going to begin going to AA and Al-Anon meetings, which I did. I was going to do everything in my being to save him.

I had to go back to the rehab facility one more time before his discharge. His counselor sat with both of us and the one thing that he asked me was, "How do you know when he is lying?" I tried answering with things he may say or do, but he stopped me and said, "You know when he is lying when his lips are moving." That statement still sticks with me. He also stated that my boyfriend needed a year before making any sudden life changes, the meetings he needed to go to, etc.

I will never forget the day I picked him up...I bought a dress just for his homecoming. I couldn't get to him fast enough. I was so excited that finally he was on the road to recovery. I felt that our life was beginning. During his stay, my kids and I took care of his dog. On the way to my boyfriend's house, we stopped by my home to pick up his dog before getting him settled back in at his place. We talked about the meetings that he needed to schedule and begin attending. I wanted the change so desperately for him. The next day I went over to see how he was doing, and I could see it—he was drinking again.

I asked him about the drinking. He wouldn't give me a straight answer and walked into the house. He came back out and got down on one knee and asked me to marry him. I knew that I needed to say no. I kept hearing what his counselor was saying about big life changes, and instead, I said yes...with instant regret. Within a week, we were screaming at each other, and the ring was back in his possession. It truly was tumultuous.

At that point, I was emotionally, physically, mentally, and spiritually exhausted. I was done with the lying, the drinking, the cheating, the ups, the downs, and the fear of stepping on a land mine, not knowing which side of him I was going to get. I was tired of distancing myself from my friends and my family, doing things I wasn't proud of, and lying to my family to spend time with him for fear of being judged. I was so frustrated with so many things. I knew that I needed to end this rollercoaster ride.

I did for a while, once again, until my grandmother passed away. We were both extremely close to her, and he would randomly visit her. I called to let him know, but he didn't answer right away, so I called again. This time he answered, and I shared the news. He said nothing and instead hung up. I was super hurt. I had been by his side for so many things and I needed just a little support. Instead, I got a text message from him stating that he didn't feel bad for me because we all wanted her dead anyway. Even now as I type those words I want to throw up. I guess I still have some healing to do.

I went to her service, and there was no sign of him. Me, the hopeless romantic, always wishing he would pull through. He called me a few days later stating that he was at the funeral home standing in the back. I could tell you every person that was in that room and he wasn't there. But because I didn't trust myself, I second-guessed myself, thinking perhaps he was, and I just didn't see him. I didn't see him because he wasn't there. I was done. There was no going back and I didn't.

He did go back into rehab. He wrote me two letters stating that he was sorry for everything he put me through. I so desperately wanted to respond but decided to leave well enough alone. I thought about him every day, hoping that he was doing well, hoping that he was happy, and wondering if I did everything that I could to help him, and finally realizing that I couldn't help him, but I could help myself. I had previously been in therapy and now it was full speed ahead. I found myself dating someone else, but it wasn't him.

As I mentioned earlier, he was a K-9 officer and had a knack for working and training animals. He shared that gift with my daughter. She had moved away from home and adopted a rescue dog. She and I had talked about how proud he would be of her and the way that she had trained her dog. He had been reaching out, and I asked if it would be okay if we stopped by. My daughter and I, along with her new pup, stopped by his home after he responded with yes. We never went inside. We hung out outside and played with her dog. She was so proud to show him the pointers that he had shared with her, which were now being shared with her dog. We stayed for about forty-five minutes and as we were getting ready to leave, I said my goodbye with a hug. That was the last time I saw him.

A few weeks had gone by, and he called one night. We talked for over an hour. He didn't tell me that he had someone living with him even when I asked. I found out when she had entered his home and spoke to him. He told her to shut up because he was on the phone working on his future. I knew that I was no longer an option for a future for him and stated that it was time for us to end that phone call. That was the last time that I spoke directly to him.

He reached out a few more times, tempting me with a baseball ticket and my favorite candy, Peanut Chews, tucked in my mailbox with a note asking me to try again. He said he would be at the baseball stadium with the other ticket waiting for me. Sounds really romantic, even now as I type it. I was so tempted, but I stayed strong and didn't go. I wanted to but knew that I had to save myself at this point. There was no going back to him. That note was dated July 25, 2013, and was the last form of communication I had with him. He passed away in August 2013. He was thirty-five years old.

I felt extremely guilty for many years, wondering if I had stayed if that would have changed our destiny. I know that I did try. I did try to save him. Unfortunately, you can't save someone who doesn't want to be saved. And realistically, at times during my relationship with him, I didn't want to save myself either. Thankfully, though, I found the strength to do the work and save myself. He taught me that.

He taught me so many lessons and continues to do so. The greatest gift he gave me was teaching me that my children were not just a responsibility. For so long I was a single parent, even when I was married. He taught me to have fun with my kids. He taught me how to be spontaneous. He taught me how to have fun doing the smallest things. He taught me how to find the bunny on the front cover of Playboy magazine (it was a competition who could find it first). He taught me not to settle for anything less than I deserve. He taught me that alcohol is not the only addiction out there; we also have addictions to people, to feelings, to situations. I was addicted to wanting to fix, wanting to help, wanting to save. (They say that the people we date are a reflection of ourselves, which explains why 95 percent of the men I dated had some sort of addiction.) I reached a point when I knew that I wasn't helping him, as much as I wanted to believe that I was. I gave myself way more power than was realistic.

This disease was stronger than him. I believe he wanted to quit drinking for us, for my kids, but he just couldn't. Despite his sickness, he had a great, great heart. I felt the magic that he was. He had a super personality and was extremely generous. He always did things to the extreme. He asked one time if he could bring the kids Silly String. I said, "Sure, why not." Well, he not only brought over four cans, but he brought over a case. He would always pick up the tab when he was out with his friends. He would say that he wanted to do it because he wanted his friends to remember when he did that for them.

I believe that he knew his life was going to end sooner rather than later. His infamous line was always, "You have a date stamped on your ass, and you aren't going to do anything to change it." Truest statement ever. He lived his life to the fullest. Unfortunately, there were a lot of demons that just would not ease up.

He fought in the war in 2001. He left a young man and came back as an adult. Although I didn't know him then, he shared his stories with me...they are not mine to tell and I will take them to the grave, but I will say that those stories were shared with me at 4 a.m. when he was in a drunken stupor because he was emotionally in so much pain. I would listen, I would try to understand, but I couldn't...I wasn't there. All I could do was hug him and pray for him that he would find the peace he so desperately wanted for his heart. I could go off on a tangent as far as the military goes, and how they don't give their soldiers the proper assistance when they come home, but I won't because the person that this story is about would say, "It is what it is."

He has been physically out of my life for almost ten years now. And it's made me realize how unhealed I still am. I shed tears on the keys of my computer for many reasons. They are for loving him, losing him, hurting him, hurting myself, allowing it to go on as long as it did, hurting friends and family, for being someone that I didn't even know, and most importantly, for taking the time to realize how far I have come and the lessons that this relationship taught me.

Even though my relationship with him brought me a lot of great memories—from the trips we took, the sunrises we watched together after being up all night talking, the funny conversations around the dinner table (thank goodness for video), the day trips (my favorite being a hike to see some waterfalls)—it also brought me a lot of heartaches that instead of processing, I buried. I/we were on a constant hamster wheel of together, not together, loving each other, hurting each other. It was a vicious cycle, and the only way of ending it was to remove myself. Addiction not only affects the individual, but it affects the family, the friends, and the people who love and care. It affects a community. It truly has a ripple effect.

I will always love this man. Our hearts collided many lifetimes ago. I believe that we have always been together in some way, shape, and form, but this lifetime his lesson for me was to teach me how to save myself—to love myself enough to leave toxic situations. The lessons were not easy, but I thank him from the bottom of my heart for that lesson...as painful as it was and sometimes continues to be. Quite often our greatest heartaches are our greatest teachers.

May your soul finally rest in peace WCM...all my love, NKH.

Nanci and WCM share an intimate moment. (photo credit: Nanci Hummer, August 2009)

"*Cause sometimes you just feel tired. Feel weak, and when you feel weak, you feel like you wanna just give up. But you gotta search within you. Try to find that inner strength. And just pull that shit out of you, and get that motivation to not give up, and not be a quitter, no matter how bad you wanna just fall flat on your face and collapse.*"

Eminem

CHAPTER FOUR

FADE TO BLACK

By Marigold Lombardo

IMAGINE YOU ARE a small child. You're three years old, and the world is so small. The people you know include your grandparents, aunts, uncles, and cousins. All you have is the family around you. At home, it's just Mommy, Daddy, Big Brother, Baby Sister, and you—a family of five. You and your brother are playing together nicely—until he takes your toy away. Being a toddler, you think *hey, that was my toy,* and you begin to cry. The moment you realize you have made a mistake, it's too late: Daddy is up. *Wait, where's Mommy?* Daddy rushes over to both of you, veins bulging, rips your brother right off the floor, slams him hard against the wall by his throat, and screams, "LEAVE YOUR SISTER ALONE!" Suddenly you're crying even harder. He turns to you. He takes his hand; big enough to cover your entire face, places his thumb and forefinger around your nose, pinches your nostrils together, and covers your mouth. His other hand firmly grasps the back of your head. The next time you attempt a breath, there is no air; only a big, coarse hand. *Daddy, I can't breathe,* you think. "Stop crying, NOW," he demands through clenched teeth.

I replayed the visions of my dad hurting my brother. I replayed the thought of suffocating. I kept feeling the warmth of my breath and tears, the vapor created by my dad's hot hand over my burning face, and my eyes bulging from fear and hysteria. I thought about it all on a loop, and then, I didn't think about it anymore. Repressed. On to the next thing. Me, my crying, and my emotions were always to blame. My mom would tell me that I was the reason my dad hit my brother. My brother agreed, and that began my career as their enemy. I was high energy and high emotion; I exploded at times. I looked like my father and my behavior attached me to him. It was tough, but I was told it could always be worse. So, I tried not to complain. I tried not to cry. At the time, I just wanted to be a good kid, you know?

We lived in a small, one-bedroom apartment above my grandparents' garage. I remember my mom calling the police to our apartment. The altercation involved both of my parents and ended in my father punching my mother's forehead. All I know was there were police at our door, and I was frightened. No matter the drama, my parents chose to stay together. My grandparents were not thrilled. My dad was bad news.

Some fun facts about my dad: he was born one year before Marshall Mathers, aka Eminem. He grew up in the projects of Easton with two siblings. As children, they did things like scream so loudly my aunt was made deaf in one ear. She was so angry with him once that she threw a butcher's knife at him, and he had a scar on his left armpit to prove it. He dropped out of high school at seventeen to become a young father. He looked like Eddie Munson, from *Stranger Things*, but with blue eyes. He could have followed Metallica on tour and become a rock star. He could have used his artistic talents to create his own cartoon show. Instead, he kept a drumstick, from a concert in 1990, tucked away in a cabinet and acted out with drugs and violence.

The next thing I knew, we were moving away from my grandparents. It was so comforting having my Nana next door—a special Italian grandmother. If it wasn't for that woman, I don't think I could have known real love at such a young age. A love like hers was fundamental to my growth. I can still smell her, and she's been gone for ten years. That kind of love. I could write a book about her love. And they took me away from her. We were in the same city, I admit it, but I was only freaking five. I memorized the route from her house to mine. If things got tough, I would make it back to her, like a Selena Gomez song.

It didn't take long for things to get tough. Parties became more frequent. My parents already knew how to throw a good party. When we lived in the apartment, my birthdays were fun for everyone. I was born in early September and the Labor Day holiday gave people an excuse to celebrate even more. I rode on the back of a motorcycle for the first time at my fourth party. And I'm pretty sure at the party before that, my cousin was conceived. My little sister and my mother were both born on October 25th. This meant Halloween-themed birthday parties for them. The point is, my parents had their own house to throw parties in now, and they were down to get down.

At one of those parties, my dad, wearing high heels and a dress with balloons for breasts, proudly taught me how to pour from a keg.

"You have to tilt the cup," he told me.

"Okay, Daddy," I replied, while someone from the party snapped a picture.

I was so happy to please them. So proud of myself for being trusted to pour from a freaking keg. And I thought the parties were fun. I thought my dad was such a good time. He had friends, he laughed out loud, and he let go. My mom danced, my dad got wasted, and they seemed happy. But he wanted to party all the time. He was living fast and dying faster. Three kids and a wife could be a drag. Hell, life could be a drag.

One night, my mom caught him looking for money in her purse. I watched from the hallway as my mom ripped her bag from his hands and sprinted toward me. I backed into the corner, out of her way, stunned. She turned to go up the stairs, and I realized that he was right behind her. They caught each other at the top of the stairs and just collapsed into each other, crying loudly. They were a trainwreck, and I still didn't know what the hell was going on.

I started kindergarten the same month I turned six. I'll just highlight some things about my school year at Paxinosa Elementary School: my mom taught me how to dance the *Macarena* and my dad brought our pet scorpion into Show and Tell. I kissed the neighbor kid, with my tongue. Yes, I was young. Anyway, somehow my dad had reconnected with his father. He was around twenty-five at the time and hadn't seen his father since he was about seven. I know, I did The Rock's famous eyebrow raise when I gathered that information, too. So, we took a trip. We drove 500 miles from Easton, Pennsylvania, to Seagrove, North Carolina. I was totally excited to take the trip until the trip turned into a perfect opportunity for my parents to start over. We were going to move to North Carolina and my parents were going to be better, together.

My first summer in North Carolina was many things; especially hot. Not just wicked hot, but grossly humid too. Maybe I was being dramatic again, but I distinctly remember the weather change and feeling sticky way too early in the morning. But the opportunity to explore nature in the warmer weather excited me. My dad encouraged us to explore things and to keep our eyes peeled. I remember the neighbors were within walking distance from the house we were sharing with my grandfather. I thought it was cool that they weren't sharing a wall with neighbors like the house in Easton.

One evening, my dad walked us over to see an alligator snapping turtle the neighbor caught. It was totally awesome; I had never seen a turtle so big. I saw hummingbirds and cardinals. And we visited the North Carolina Zoo for the first time as a family. Things like that and my parents' seeming optimism helped make the move more bearable.

It was 1997 when first grade began at Seagrove Elementary School. I was set on never having a southern accent, never curving the ends of my letters, and never, ever loving anything 500 miles away from my Nana. We stayed with my grandfather and his partner until we could get a place of our own. My mom started working the night shift at Walmart, and my dad worked as a mechanic at a place called Thomas Tire.

In second grade, we moved from our grandfather's modular home in Seagrove to our single-wide trailer on a lot in Randleman. Again: What up, Eminem? Thankfully, the move didn't mean a school change. By third grade, my mother became a Jehovah's Witness. This meant that she had a few new rules for us and some attendance expectations and she was done smoking cigarettes. They had smoked my whole life, so I never really thought about it ending. I was happy for her. I was also happy that she allowed me to dress up like Martha Jefferson and tell an audience that Thomas had a talking parrot in a President's Day show. She told me it was good to know history even if we weren't going to participate in politics. I was less enthused to sit out from the Valentine's Day party at school and no longer celebrate holidays. My dad was totally down with not celebrating holidays because that meant money wasn't spent on them. He said he missed us when we were away from him.

Things at home seemed quiet. My mom cleaned and studied. When she wasn't cleaning someone else's house, she was cleaning ours. She cleaned constantly. I'm serious. I knew what immaculate meant in terms of cleanliness at a very young age and totally resent it still. My dad came home from work and chilled, drinking beer every night. He would lay on the couch in his tighty-whities and socks, and watch shows like *The Simpsons, 60 Minutes, Law and Order,* and *NBC Nightly News.* We knew all our neighbors, we had a trampoline, and we learned that my dad treated dogs like crap too. Although he hit more walls than living things those days.

People still came to our house and family came to visit occasionally, but the parties pretty much stopped. I learned to make myself scarce. I could never have a conversation at home without my mouth getting me into trouble. School became the place where I really wanted to talk, and that got me into trouble too. I just loved being in school. I was happy to achieve and even happier to not need help from my parents. They had their own problems. At home, I was either in my room, quietly listening to music, or outside, so the house could stay clean for my mother. And during the summer, my sister and I would go to Easton to stay with our Nana.

We moved again. This time, I was finishing fifth grade. I remember my mom taking us to see our new house. She let us walk around. We were confused at first, and she then asked us what we thought about it being ours. It was awesome for them. They were buying a home. The house was in a new school district and the school had just been built. I would be a part of the first sixth-grade class attending Uwharrie Middle School. My parents allowed me a sleep-over to say goodbye to my friends from elementary school, and then at the end of the school year, I left for Pennsylvania. That was the summer I thought I was old enough to have a summer fling. I kissed a boy who could speak only Spanish, and I thought I was in love.

In the new house, everything fell apart. I finally learned everything—the bottles, cans, kegs, lies, cheating, mood swings, the moving, moving, moving. I thought my parents were just crazy. I understood crazy. I was crazy. But it was always more than that. I remember smelling marijuana, but my mom tolerated it, and we didn't talk about it. I viewed it as something that my dad needed because I noticed it relaxed him. But then he picked up a weekend job as a bouncer in a small nightclub, on the border of Virginia and North Carolina. Shortly after that, he started behaving like marijuana was no longer what he wanted. I remember my mom commenting on the smell of burning plastic being a trigger for my dad to run out for crack. He was smoking crack, getting drunk, and losing his head, and I hated it. Alcohol, marijuana, crack. Whatever he was doing, I hated it all.

Then, finally, and after a long journey, my mom decided she wanted a divorce. I could write a fat old book about the two of them, but at that time, her book about their relationship had ended. She tried to leave him, and he really lost his mind. He had a shotgun, one he taught us all to shoot, and he held it up to his face. He told my mom he would kill himself if she left him. She sent us outside for that one. Not too long after that, she pulled off onto the side of a road and told us she was going to leave him, without us.

He brought another woman around right away. He drank and did whatever drugs he was doing. He showed up at my mom's apartment and glued her locks. He drove her down in his F150 while she was on her way to my school. Crazy, I know, and this is just a highlight. On the bright side, I was allowed to play sports. I hadn't been allowed to since my mom converted, so when my coach offered to get me home from practice, my dad said yes. I did anything I could to avoid home. He tried everything to avoid home too.

One night I was packing for my yearly trip to Easton when he told me to make sure enough clothes were packed to move in with my mom when I returned to North Carolina. I was taken off guard by that but, being the stubborn teen I was, I made sure I packed enough clothes. When he came in later to apologize or take back his words, he was hurt to see that I had followed through. He lunged at me in anger and his tiny (in comparison to the two of us) girlfriend tried to stop him. Acting restrained behind her small arms, he told me to leave that night. It felt as if looking at me reminded him of himself and he just couldn't look at me any longer. I went to my mom's condo and started my life without my dad.

That summer, Easton was the place to stop thinking of home. My grandparents gave us freedom if we behaved. My cousin and I spent a lot of time playing cards and listening to music. I spent time with my crazy aunt, who let me do anything I wanted. With her support, I lost my virginity to the same kid I had kissed in kindergarten. It wasn't romantic, but I didn't want to go home.

On the way back to North Carolina, my mom told me we were going to stay in Phoenix for a little while, as she was figuring things out. That was code for "My boyfriend is really important to me right now." When their love affair hit a roadblock, we ended up driving from Arizona back to North Carolina. My mom, now down to nothing, had decided to move back to Pennsylvania. Then she made the impossible choice to leave my siblings behind. My sister really didn't have a choice but to stay with my dad, as the fight would have been horrendous. So that way, they each got a daughter. My brother, who was sixteen, didn't want to live with our dad and refused to leave his school and girlfriend, so he moved in with his friend. Then, my mom all but sold our souls to afford the ride from North Carolina to Pennsylvania, where we were going to restart our lives, again.

The next time I heard from my dad was around the same time I told my mom I was pregnant, at fifteen (by the guy who didn't speak English—who I lost my virginity to). My dad's new wife was pregnant too; our pregnancies were only four months apart. True story, my little sister came in September of 2006 and my daughter was born in January of 2007. He called me some derogatory names for being in a relationship with a Mexican man, and that was all for a while. I know I went to visit him before I graduated from high school in 2009 and I remember he (surprisingly) sent me $100 toward books for my first semester of college.

Later, when I was pregnant with my second child, at nineteen, he told me that I was going to rot in hell with my unborn child. The next day, I kid you not, there was an accident. He was getting into his vehicle, which at the time held a propane tank in the back seat. Just as he lit his cigarette; it was too late. An unknown leak had occurred, and the inside of the car exploded. He suffered third-degree burns and was hospitalized. Upon discharge, he was sent home with prescription painkillers.

Ten months after my son was born, I received the phone call that my dad had died. It was June 10, 2011.

He made it to forty. He lived fast, and he died young. At the funeral, my mom had to take over. His wife was dressed in her wedding gown. Completely dazed, she told everyone she vowed "in life and in death" while wearing that dress for the first time, so it seemed fitting. She sat outside, chain-smoking, while my mom accepted condolences. During the service, they allowed people to share small anecdotes about him. Then I remember crying my eyes out as they played "Fade to Black" by Metallica, per his request, and then performed a 21-gun salute.

My dad died an alcoholic and a substance abuser. His mental health was in shambles all his life and his coping mechanisms were rarely healthy. When I think of my time with him, I'm grateful for the happy moments that stand out in my mind. He would make us play football as a family, he would wrestle with us, and he would so annoyingly request that I rub and scratch his feet. His laugh was infectious. He was so silly. I remember him performing a "Fat Man Dance" for a local radio station. He was an artist; he even created his own cartoon character named Gus. People would pay him to sketch portraits of their loved ones. He taught me how to color with Crayola crayons (they're made in Easton). He would sit at the dining room table and create war scenes using Play-Doh and our old toy soldiers. He loved action movies like *Lethal Weapon* and *Tango and Cash* and war movies like *Platoon*. He loved anything with Mel Gibson. We watched *Braveheart, Signs*, and *The Patriot* all the time.

Everything was mixed up for him early in life. Just imagine the kind of sadness he must have experienced to pick a song for his own funeral. I know people do it, but he was thirteen when he chose it. Imagine living with the guilt of what happened at the beginning of this essay. He kept such strong emotions buried inside, never risking vulnerability. He never sought help of any kind. We never discussed anything as a family. My mom had strong religious beliefs and my dad watched the news every single day, yet we never discussed anything. After the big outbursts, the violence, the terrible days, and the even more terrifying nights, my parents never tried to help us figure things out. I wanted explanations. I didn't understand why he wanted to be high. I didn't understand why he was so violent. I was confused about why she stayed with him for so long. I was confused about everything.

Shortly after my father's death, my Nana died too. Two of his siblings passed away after lifelong struggles with addiction and mental illness, as well. I learned to self-deprecate. I wanted so badly to be happy but inside I was angry. Hell, I spent so long being pissed off that I honestly didn't know how I could see straight sometimes. I was degraded and physically assaulted, hit with fists or events so often that I felt loss, or I felt lost. Sadness and darkness surrounded me.

Despite it all, I show my children kindness. We moved to North Carolina in 2014. I started taking my kids to the zoo almost as soon as we arrived and then as often as possible. We paint, we draw with chalk, and when we color with crayons, I tell them who taught me how every time. We even say "Yes, Ma'am," "No, Sir," and "Y'all." We have obligatory movie nights that almost always star Drew Barrymore, Adam Sandler, or Zac Efron. Laughing helps with my depression, and I still struggle with that. But I will never stop working to break the cycle. My kids will know that mental health is constantly at risk, just like sobriety. Addiction is real, and it's not just the addict that gets messed up, but the whole family too. I will do everything I can to prevent my kids from experiencing the same path I did as a child.

"Character cannot be developed in ease and quiet. Only through experience of trial and suffering can the soul be strengthened, ambition inspired, and success achieved."

Helen Keller

CHAPTER FIVE

THE GIRL WITH THE WEIGHT OF THE WORLD IN HER HANDS

(Indigo Girls song)

*By Sherry Cooper
as told to Casey J.*

August 13, 2015—a day I will remember for the rest of my life. It is the day I lost my eldest daughter, Emily Jade Stark, to a drug overdose in Sarasota, Florida.

I texted Jade early in the day because I knew she had a doctor's appointment. When I finally managed to reach her, she sounded wasted on the phone. She told me she wasn't going to make the appointment in time and would reschedule for the following day.

That evening, Jade's three-year-old son, Tristin (whom I adopted), fell asleep around 6 p.m., which was unusual for him, but I didn't think anything of it at the time. I thought to myself, "Hey, I finally get to relax on the sofa for a little bit before bed." Right around 7 p.m., Tristin woke up, screaming. I assumed he was experiencing night terrors. He was screaming and crying as if someone was physically hurting him. It lasted for at least twenty minutes. I tried my best to console him, but it didn't help as much as it usually did. I decided to take him outside for some fresh air and eventually, he calmed down. I put him back to bed, and he fell asleep.

Around 9 p.m., a police officer appeared at my front door. My dog, who usually barked at strangers, practically glued himself to my leg and didn't make a peep. The officer told me that my daughter had passed away from an accidental overdose around 7 p.m. (the time Tristin woke up screaming and crying). I remember saying "No. NO. NO!" I walked over to my couch with my dog still attached to my leg. I couldn't stop crying. That night, I could barely sleep without crying. I kept thinking about everything we had been through together—all of the ups and downs—and now, it was over.

In November 2005, Jade was in a terrible car accident in which she totaled the car. A doctor prescribed OxyContin for the neck pain she was experiencing. Over the next several months, she totaled two more cars while driving high. The doctor gradually increased her dosage to 80 mg. I called her doctor and told him not to give her any more pills. I'm not a nasty woman, but he knew I meant business. So, he stopped prescribing them, forcing Jade to start doctor shopping for her next fix. Eventually, she turned to the streets for cheaper and more potent substances.

The drugs transformed my daughter into someone I barely recognized. Jade was an amazing and beautiful child. When she was growing up, people always commented on her caramel-colored eyes and suggested I get her involved in modeling (I never did). She had so much going for her. I wanted my little girl back, but the drugs stole her from me.

Sadly, I knew where her substance abuse stemmed from. My deceased ex-husband was abusive and volatile and also suffered from addiction. The domestic violence heavily affected my kids, so we went to therapy to help them cope. It is safe to say, they had a very tumultuous childhood. And as we all know, drugs provide a (mostly) blissful escape from reality.

In her 20s, Jade began dating a man, and they did heavy drugs together. Eventually, Jade got pregnant, and on March 13, 2012, Tristin was born addicted to opiates (Neonatal Abstinence Syndrome). The poor baby had at least seven different drugs in his system. Back then, the hospitals didn't allow mothers to breastfeed their babies to help wean them off the drugs. So, Tristin went through a 72-hour withdrawal and then was treated in the neonatal intensive care unit.

Tristin was on four different medications for twenty-eight days. When he was released, the state put him in a foster home. As soon as I learned this, I hired an attorney, and I was granted custody two weeks later, on April 25, 2012. I've been caring for him since he was six weeks old, and now he's ten.

Unfortunately, Tristin suffered from many different health issues with intermittent reflux and diarrhea being the most prominent ones. I took him to a chiropractor for adjustments. I picked up a supply of breastmilk at the birthing center. This milk was clean and drug-free. Once he started drinking it, I immediately noticed improvements. It was like night and day. His color changed. Everything about him changed. He still has issues to this day, but overall, he's doing much better.

Jade and Tristin's father refused to participate in the parenting programs offered to help reunite parents with their children. They terminated their parental rights. It took me one year to adopt Tristin. I adopted him when he was two years old, and it never should have taken that long. Playing the role of both grandma and mother poses many challenges, but I'm doing the best I can. My goal was, and still is, to keep Tristin safe and to provide him with unconditional love.

In 2013, Jade was arrested and placed in jail for thirty days. When I picked her up from jail, she looked healthy. Unfortunately, she chose her friends and drugs once again. She ended up pregnant for a second time. At some point, she told me she was going to sell her baby. In November 2014, Jade's daughter was born addicted to opiates, but she recovered in the neonatal intensive care unit. She was adopted by a family friend. I am grateful she has a loving family to grow up in, although it was heartbreaking for Jade at the time.

Every now and then, Jade would come to my house to see Tristin, but I really didn't like her around him when she was wasted. Her behavior was unpredictable. She would be calm one minute and then blow up the next. He didn't need to see his mother in that condition. It wasn't fair to him, and her presence made me nervous. I didn't want to risk losing my youngest son, Joshua, and grandson, Tristin, to the state for communicating with and helping Jade. Her drug use got her in so much trouble, and Tristin didn't need to be a part of that. I needed to establish healthy boundaries for all of us.

One day, in March 2015, Jade called me and said she had been in a car crash, and someone she was doing drug deals with broke her jaw. I remember thinking *What the hell is going on?* Then again, in May 2015, Jade called me and said another man broke her jaw. She refused to go to the hospital, but I forced her to go. She needed medical treatment as soon as possible.

On June 4, 2015, she was put in a medically induced coma. The doctors wired her jaw shut. At this time, she was diagnosed with Hepatitis C. A part of me was relieved that she would be in the hospital for a short period because she needed time to heal. I was also afraid if the hospital released her, someone would kill her.

The doctors woke Jade up on the 19th day. I went to visit her. She was on pain medications and fentanyl patches, so she was in a good mood. And for the first time in a very long time, we talked. And then we talked some more. We attempted to heal and repair our relationship. She told me she was mentally ill and needed help. I was hopeful. I gave her resources and referrals in Sarasota. I really thought I was going to get my daughter back.

And then on August 13, 2015, drugs ended her short life. She was only thirty-one years old. The toxicology report showed she had fentanyl-laced cocaine, Roxicodone, Xanax, Gabapentin, and Dilaudid in her system when she passed. Since most of my family and her father lived in Louisville, Kentucky, we flew her casket back there to be buried.

I remember mentally preparing myself for the long drive back to Kentucky to bury my daughter. I finally managed to fall asleep that night, and that's when it happened—eighty hours after Jade passed. It was around 7 a.m., and I was in bed asleep, or at least I thought I was asleep. It must have been some form of sleep paralysis. I felt as if a lightning bolt hit my chest—like a sword stabbed me. Oddly enough, the sensation didn't hurt. In my consciousness, I thought I was dying. And then it felt like someone was pouring hot oil all over my body. I couldn't move or open my eyes. But then I felt this unexplainable joy sweep over me. I opened my eyes, and I saw a giant golden glowing sign that said "TODAY" in my consciousness. It felt like the day my baby girl, Jade, was born. Love was restored to my body. Maybe the lightning bolt to my chest fueled me up with the strength and love I would need to care for Tristin. It was a beautiful moment, and I enjoyed every second of it. I felt as ready as one can be to say goodbye.

At her funeral, I learned from my younger sister that from January to March 2015, Jade had overdosed five times while staying with my family in Kentucky. Narcan had to be administered one time, and because Narcan killed her high, she was back out on the streets shortly after that, searching for drugs. Within a few short months, Jade returned to Sarasota, where she eventually lost her battle with addiction.

I still have sadness in my heart. I still have waves of grief that come and go. But in the last three years, I've come to appreciate all the joy I had with Jade. She brought so much beauty into my life, and I remember that more than the pain—similar to childbirth.

Even though Jade is no longer physically here with us, I still feel her presence. She is an angel watching over us. I ask her all the time to help me raise Tristin, and I know she's supporting me. It gives me peace of mind knowing she's no longer in any pain. She suffered from addiction for ten years, and now she's free from her disease. I fought so hard to save her, but she had to want to save her life; I couldn't do it for her.

No parent should ever have to go through the pain of losing a child, but unfortunately, more and more parents are losing their children to overdoses. The amount of fentanyl pouring into this country is overwhelming. Fentanyl is killing them instantly. This world is dying. The system is broken. We are a throw-away society, and we need to change that. We need a community-based support system for these people. We can't hide behind these stories anymore. The shame—the stigma—they need to go. These people need love. They need compassion. We need to get them off the streets. We can't let them slip through the cracks and into the gutter. We need to speak out and be the change this world so desperately needs.

Jade Stark (photo credit: Sherry Cooper, October 2004)

The Dark Place
The Dark Place is a place that makes you feel all ALONE
Because you are there with strangers who have taken
You from your HOME
You can't see your Mother or Father because one
of them has done Wrong
The Dark Place is a Place Where You Have to be STRONG

By Jade Stark
Home of the Innocents
August 30, 1996

"It is by going down into the abyss that we recover the treasures of life. Where you stumble, there lies your treasure."

Joseph Campbell

CHAPTER SIX

H.O.P.E.

By Officer Sam Hooper
as told to Casey J.

"SHOW OF HANDS, please. Who here has been personally affected or knows someone who has been affected by the current opioid epidemic?"

I gaze at the large group of people of all ages looking back at me. Every single hand reaches high into the air. Unfortunately, it doesn't surprise me. In this day and age, it's almost to be expected.

The opioid epidemic is so rampant, it has spread like wildfire throughout our country—destroying the lives of families everywhere. So, what can we do to try to combat this? We can offer people the tools they need to be prepared. We may not be able to stop a person from using drugs, but we can at least teach families what signs to watch for and how to properly administer life-saving treatment.

I am currently a police officer with thirty years of service, and I teach classes as part of the H.O.P.E. (Heroin Opioid Prevention Education) program for families of loved ones who suffer from substance use disorder. Many substance abusers live double lives and attempt to hide their addiction from their family members. Parents, siblings, and spouses will tell me that they had no idea there was even a problem until their loved one was arrested for drugs or worse—dead from an overdose.

During these classes, I inform families about the signs to look for, such as tiny cotton balls (which are used for filtering out any impurities before preparing liquid for a hypodermic needle); burned bottoms of spoons with dried white residue on top; and missing shoelaces (which are used as tourniquets while injecting and then untied and removed). I also discuss the importance of having Narcan readily available to reverse an opioid overdose (this is supplied upon request at a local pharmacy). While on the job, we go through a lot of Narcan—one time we administered Narcan six times in one week just on my shift. I have noticed that we've been receiving fewer emergency calls since families now know how to administer life-saving medication to their loved ones. Sadly, it's becoming part of the norm.

On top of the overdose cases, we have the ones where the parents file reports regarding their children stealing their TVs, jewelry, and other valuables to sell for drug money. We inform these parents that we can charge their children with theft, but most parents decline. We then advise that they admit their children into a rehab facility, but most refuse to go. It is essentially enabling them by putting up with their behavior. At some point, you need to put your foot down and say enough is enough. I know it's hard, but it has to be done. The abuser needs to know their behavior and actions will not be tolerated, and that they need to seek professional treatment. Addiction affects the whole family, not just the substance abuser.

When I entered the police force in 1993, crack cocaine was out of control. Movies such as *Colors* and *Boyz n the Hood* portrayed the crack epidemic and the violence that went along with it perfectly. Drug users were stealing anything to buy a $5 rock. They weren't taking care of their kids. People were killing each other just to get their next fix. There were a record number of homicides across the country. Now, fast forward twenty years, and opioids—OxyContin, Percocet, heroin—have replaced crack cocaine as the number one drug of choice.

I want to share a few stories with you to hopefully deter you from trying these mind-altering drugs and to show you that addiction doesn't discriminate. One time, we had a man down with a needle sticking out of his arm. We used Narcan on him and thirty seconds later, he came to. Normally, one would imagine that the person would be grateful to us for saving his life. Nope. He was upset and angry with us for ruining his high. This reaction is very common among opioid users.

About six years ago, we received a call about two people who overdosed in a car. I arrived on the scene first. Two young women, dressed nicely, were sitting in the front seats, barely breathing. I pulled them out of the car, administered Narcan, and performed sternum rubs. They finally came around. The first girl was receptive to my questions. She told me they grounded up and snorted Percocets. The second girl denied all of it. She claimed she was at work. She didn't realize she was outside of her car, on the sidewalk, coming out of an overdose. I experienced two more overdoses with the second girl within the next six months. I remember telling her, "You're gonna do this and nobody will be around to save you." She was 21 years old at the time. She did reach out months later and told me she was finally clean, which was a positive story for a change. Unfortunately, not everybody makes it out alive.

My buddy lost his son to a heroin overdose; he was injured, prescribed oxy for the pain, and within a short period of time, was hooked on heroin. Nearly every story I've ever heard begins with "They had surgery and they were prescribed opioids, which eventually led to heroin." When you look at the big picture, it makes sense—$30 per pill on the street or $10 for a bag of heroin? Drug users are going to choose the latter. Similar high for much less money.

The first high is always the best. Users will continuously chase that initial high, but it will never be as good as the first. Eventually, they build up a tolerance. They require more and more to achieve that much anticipated high. But nowadays, users are taking an extreme risk of buying illegal drugs off the streets. They have to hope they're getting legitimate heroin and not fentanyl or xylazine (an animal tranquilizer, which can cause many dangerous side effects, including necrotic skin ulcers) mixed in.

The worst part about the fentanyl crisis is that dealers are mixing it with other drugs, and the people selling it don't even care that they're killing people. It's a multi-million dollar business. It's a guaranteed job, and their primary concern is making money. There will always be a supply and demand. If one customer dies from an overdose, there will always be another one to replace them. The bodies will continue to pile up while the money pours in.

Over the years, I've become numb to seeing dead bodies (homicides, overdoses, suicides, etc.). There have been THAT many. I learned to function through it. In my head, it's just another call. I knew what I was getting myself into when I decided, at sixteen, that I wanted to be the first police officer in my family. I was fortunate enough to attend SWAT school, sniper school, helicopter rappel school, K-9 school, tactical medical school, and three different narcotic schools. I loved the adrenaline that came with the job. I enjoyed knowing that when we were called, we were going after the worst criminals and getting them off the street. I wanted to help keep people safe, but it can be challenging.

I'll admit that we do get frustrated with repeat offenders. It used to be if a person overdosed, we did an emergency evaluation at the hospital. We would attempt to force them to get help. Eventually, the hospital staff told us to stop bringing them in—that these people just wanted to get high and that they weren't trying to kill themselves. So now, when we receive an overdose call, we give them Narcan, and they sign a release form saying they don't want to go to the hospital, and that's that. They just want to be left alone so they can go off and get high again. Over the years, I would say only one or two ever went to the hospital. The vast majority don't want to go. They're mainly upset that the Narcan and CPR we perform ruined their high.

I hope that sooner rather than later, we can get this situation under control and prevent more lives from being lost. We need to educate and raise awareness on this critical issue.

Officer Sam Hooper (photo credit: Sam Hooper, 2015)

"If you can quit for a day, you can quit for a lifetime."

Benjamin Alire Sáenz

CHAPTER SEVEN

A QUICK FIX

By Captain John Mazzeo
as told to Casey J.

I MAGINE WALKING INTO a house, finding 200 syringes, an obscene amount of heroin baggies, and a woman in her fifties, with one pant leg on and panties pulled down, lying dead on the floor from an overdose. She had been deceased for at least ten hours based on lividity and rigor mortis. Come to find out, the two men using with her were having sex with her postmortem. The father and son were as high as the sky and had absolutely no perception as to what they were doing. It was one of the more disturbing cases I witnessed during my forty-eight years working as a police officer (thirty of those spent patrolling the streets of Easton, Pennsylvania). Unfortunately, overdoses are becoming more and more common, not only in our county but throughout the country.

I no longer patrol the streets, but when I did, we would typically receive calls in the early morning hours from passersby, friends, or relatives discovering users passed out behind the wheel of a car. The Patrol Division would investigate and find the engine turned on, the person's foot on the brake pedal, and a needle still stuck in their arm. If the doors were locked, we would break in to save their lives. Nine times out of ten, they would wake up and come at us, swinging, because we killed their high. In a separate incident, I had an individual overdose on heroin three times during one eight-hour shift.

Narcotics are very easy to overdose on. They suppress your breathing and can potentially suffocate you to death. I can't stress enough just how dangerous these drugs are. Ingesting, snorting, smoking, injecting—none of these methods are safe. People need to abstain altogether.

When I worked as a patrol sergeant and later as a patrol lieutenant,

I dealt with many cases of people strung out on phencyclidine (PCP), cocaine, crack, LSD (acid), you name it. Heroin seemed to be the most popular drug of choice, but even that had its lulls. I do recall a couple of bizarre encounters with people high on angel dust, which is slang for PCP. These users tend to be more aggressive and delusional/paranoid. One man was climbing a telephone pole, so we attempted to get him down. Once his feet hit the ground, he came at us with razor blades.

Another night, we found a young girl high on PCP. I believe she said her drink was spiked with it. Given that PCP dissolves easily in liquid, and a lot of addicts combine it with alcohol for a sedative effect, that scenario was quite possible. She was outside, not wearing any pants or panties, in three-degree weather, groveling around on the ground like a chicken. We attempted to restrain her without hurting her, but she was as strong as a bear. Eventually, we managed to get her to the hospital, but it was no easy task.

It can be very risky handling people under the influence of mind-altering drugs. It's a hard job. You either do it or you quit. A lot of cops end up quitting. Sometimes the job calls you; you don't always call the job. Police work is all I've ever known. It became my passion. My grandfather was a cop for thirty-five years in Easton. When my dad came home from World War II, he worked as a police officer for twenty-seven years in Easton. When he retired in 1973, I took my exam to enter the force. My family has a century of service with the city of Easton. I love my job, but it has its downsides.

You can watch shows and listen to stories, but you'll never know what it's like until you're totally immersed in it. I've witnessed many overdoses over the course of my career, and after a while, I've become calloused to them. But that doesn't mean they didn't affect me at all. Everybody forms their own way of dealing with those traumas—physically, emotionally, or both. I was never one to go home to my family and say, "Guess what happened today?" Now, if my ex-wife or daughter asked me a question, I would answer it, but for the most part, I internalized all of it. I put it in a little box on an imaginary shelf somewhere and didn't think about it. Sometimes, something would trigger it, forcing me to think about it, but then I would tuck it back away on that imaginary shelf. I've been lucky that a lot of things I experienced really didn't bother me. It just appears that over the years things have only gotten worse.

I would say about fifteen or twenty years ago, we received several calls a week about overdoses. Lately, there have been a hell of a lot more. In most cases, we have to provide direct care on the street. We have more tools now to handle these cases properly as opposed to years ago. The paramedics carry Narcan and administer it to the user to reverse the overdose. Sometimes the user will acquire high-quality heroin or heroin laced with a stronger opioid, which we call a "hot shot," and they overdose on their initial use without intending to do so. A lot of people end up killing themselves. You just don't know what you're getting on the street. None of it is safe, and you're gambling with your life. It's like Russian roulette. Who would want to play that game? I know I wouldn't. Fortunately, for some, we do revive them in time and send them to a local hospital for medical treatment.

The user is evaluated, and if suicide was attempted, (what we call a) 302 is initiated, and the person is involuntarily committed to a psychiatric facility for up to seventy-two hours. There is a hearing and testimony to determine whether further treatment is needed. If we catch casual users using illicit drugs, we arrest them and place them into a system for counseling. We understand these people need help. We try to do the best we can by them. The problem is getting them to seek and stay in professional treatment.

Substance abusers face two options: they either hospitalize themselves or overdose. Unfortunately, most are resistant to voluntary or mandated facilities. The facilities just don't work. Sometimes, imprisonment may be the only real solution to help users get clean. What they decide to do once they're released from prison is up to them. Some of these abusers are not only a danger to themselves but to others as well. It affects every aspect of the user's life.

People from all walks of life can and do suffer from substance use disorder, which is a mental illness. The brain is rewired, and the primary goal is obtaining and abusing a substance or several different substances to achieve a much-desired high. Drugs and alcohol negatively impact the whole family. People's personalities change—care for children changes. Everybody involved suffers.

The bulk of abusers are willing to do anything to purchase their drug of choice—sell drugs, theft, prostitution, commit violent crimes, etc. They are so focused on getting their fix, the sky is the limit. They are driven by it. And it's just not illicit drugs being abused, but prescription medications as well. It appears now more and more people are finding comfort in prescription drugs to ease any mental or physical pain, or simply to get high.

My daughter works as a counselor, and most of her clients just want to be prescribed medications to cope with their problems. They don't have the will to work on them. Her goal is to get to the root cause of their issues, not offer temporary solutions. She lost three or four clients recently because she refused to suggest prescription medications. There are pills for everything. Everybody wants a quick fix. Although prescription medications seem to be the "in" thing now, I feel we have an even bigger problem on our hands—fentanyl—a synthetic opioid 50 times stronger than heroin.

I was a canine handler, a SWAT commander/primary firearms use and force instructor, and a captain of field services, and I worked for SAIC and Leidos Corporation, specializing in weapons of mass destruction. It's safe to say I've experienced a lot during my time on the force, but nothing worries me more than the amount of fentanyl flooding into our country from China and Mexico. I would consider fentanyl to be the deadliest substance in the world. Only a minute amount is needed to kill you.

In 2022, enough fentanyl was seized at the border to kill every American in the United States. Just think about how much more fentanyl snuck in under the radar. We have to assume any illicit drug dealt on the street contains fentanyl. It's poison. Fentanyl is poisoning and killing people of all ages, races, and genders, and it's doing it in record numbers. We need to increase awareness and educate people on the dangers of illicit and prescription drug use. More lives will be lost if we don't act now.

"When you get into a tight place and everything goes against you, till it seems you could not hang on a minute longer, never give up then, for that is just the place and time that the tide will turn."

Harriet Beecher Stowe

CHAPTER EIGHT

A MENTAL HEALTH CRISIS

*By Al Bassetti, Marigold Lombardo, Toni, and Lisa
as told to Marigold Lombardo and Casey J.*

(This chapter includes several personal reflections from medical health professionals who wanted to provide insights about their experiences with substance use disorder.)

AL BASSETTI, Director of Hunterdon Behavioral Health's Emergency Services

I DECIDED TO work in the mental health field when I was in high school. I started working, with my first job, in private residential treatment in 1979. I've worked at Hunterdon for the last thirty-one years, and I started here in crisis services, along with outpatient services. There is no daily routine. There are periods of boredom punctuated by absolute chaos. We see patients of all ages. Over the last few years, mostly due to COVID, we've seen an increase in severity and acuity in behavioral health and addiction, but not necessarily a spike in overall volume. I've noticed an uptick in mental health and addiction issues in adolescents and adults.

We have a comprehensive service line here at Hunterdon Medical Center, which is a not-for-profit community hospital in Flemington, New Jersey. We have a fourteen-bed voluntary unit, which treats mental illness and provides detox for alcohol and benzodiazepines. Our average length of stay for our inpatient unit is five days. The medical center provides a day hospital for chronically, persistently mentally ill patients, who can be treated in the milieu, using medication and group therapy for many months.

We also offer an acute partial program where patients meet five days a week for group therapy sessions, and an intensive outpatient program, which is available in the evenings for three hours per night, three days per week. Intensive outpatient can serve adults, adolescents, addictions, and mental health issues. It is particularly attractive for those adults who work and need something after hours, or adolescents who need treatment after school hours. Intensive outpatient can last anywhere from four to six weeks. An advanced practice nurse and a psychotherapist are available to tend to the patients during these sessions.

We offer regular addiction services and regular outpatient services for those using and abusing cocaine, marijuana, hallucinogens, opioids, etc. Patients can be treated here for either a straight or dual diagnosis. We offer one-on-one psychotherapy for addiction, and both men's and women's groups for issues dealing with trauma, anxiety, etc.

Our grant-funded Opioid Overdose Recovery Program involves peers making contact with overdose victims and encouraging the users to stay sober. Harm reduction is a large part of our work. Our Navigator (a case manager) aims to get them the proper medical care they require. We want them to stay sober and take back control of their lives. The peers are individuals who are stable now but went through the system for their own mental health issues. This approach is an evidenced-based practice that seems to be more productive for this population, which is more amenable to accepting guidance from peers as opposed to hearing advice from professionals who haven't experienced it themselves.

MARIGOLD LOMBARDO, Former Phlebotomist

In 2020, one of the last places people wanted to work was in a hospital. When COVID first hit, I worked as a phlebotomist in the Emergency Department (ED) in High Point, North Carolina. Not necessarily the tourist capital of the world, but totally touristy. It is known for its Furniture Market and houses the "World's Largest Chest of Drawers." COVID changed everything inside the ED. At first, the lobby was empty. I mean tumbleweeds-blowing-in-the-desert empty. People were shook, really shook, like Shaggy-and-Scooby-just-saw-a-ghost shook. Scared-ass people all around us, and we still had to show up if we wanted a paycheck. I mean, there was a time when management was being sent home, people were leaving their twelve-hour shifts early, people were calling out, people quit. It was a lot to take in for those of us who kept showing up and working at the hospital.

The lobby was rid of the normal, everyday hustle and bustle. The regulars—simple cases like pregnancy testing, stubbed toes, patients who were non-compliant with other medical providers, the injured but not emergent, all found somewhere else to be. And that was nuts! All of a sudden, the ED was empty. We went back in time to when the ED was used for real emergencies. Real emergencies meant people were dying. So, although the lobby was quiet, the ED kept running, bracing for the impact of COVID.

Once COVID hit the Piedmont Triad (this is what the region of North Carolina is called), the lobby exploded. Those precious moments when we could show up to work and breathe were over. We were running...for our lives. We were collecting so much blood by the end of 2020 that they offered phlebotomists a course to start IVs on patients; it was insane. Normally, nurses were the only people allowed to start IVs on patients, but once COVID hit, we were given the opportunity to train and certify for the skill set as well. And when the shelters minimized capacity? Homeless patients who couldn't get into the shelters ended up on the streets or in the ED. Maintain a six-foot distance? Patients were elbow to elbow, and no one could have visitors. We had a jam-packed hospital, a slammed emergency department, and a full lobby. There were wait times of over twelve hours. Nurses who normally worked only in the ED, who were used to stabilizing patients and sending them on to other units, had to become floor nurses in a makeshift ICU (Intensive Care Unit) straight out of the ED. They had rounds to do on patients, now, they had to order meals and distribute meds too; it was wild. We had more and more patients. More and more time spent with patients, a full behavioral health unit, and a line out the door with patients searching for help.

So, the routine for someone looking for detox, rehabilitation, or a psychiatric evaluation was such: check-in, provide urine and blood (a basic urinalysis, drug screen, CBC and BMP/CMP, which are Complete Blood Count and Basic/Complete Metabolic Panel, just a baseline health status so that there is no reason to be treated in the ED before entering the locked Behavioral Health Unit), then out to the lobby (pending no suicidal ideation, in which case the patient should not be left alone) until there was an available bed. That means a person suffering from some form of mental illness went from triage to me. I was a mother of five at the time, married to a man in recovery, and handling my own trauma, and I was there to stick a needle in the patient's arm.

To share my experience is nothing less than humbling. I was always someone who said addiction was a choice, but I honestly didn't understand enough. I met each patient with fresh, non-judgmental eyes, on what could have been one of the hardest days of their lives. I came in contact with people from all walks of life, struggling in different ways with mental illness and substance abuse. There were times IV drug users would come in and offer to help me with my job or joke about working with me. I honestly loved the opportunity to test my skills with "hard sticks" and the stories that almost always came with them. I hated to see when a bad batch of whatever drug brought overdoses into the department left and right. I hated to see the mental illness grow in certain patients who were also homeless.

As things got rough with COVID, patients grew more weary. They lost respect for staff. I remember a patient, for the first time in my almost ten years as a phlebotomist, who actually grabbed my arm while I held a needle in it. He was a drug abuser and a regular patient. I had drawn his blood numerous times before, and he had never been physical with me, but he was in an altered state of mind and believed I intended to hurt him. On another occasion, a patient became belligerent in triage and was escorted to my phlebotomy chair by two security guards. While he allowed me to draw his blood, he spoke to the security guards like they were worthless, and then when I withdrew the needle, he told me I was worthless too and attempted to buck at me. Security restrained him, and after searching his belongings, they found a machete in his backpack. I no longer felt safe in the workplace, but I kept working.

I spent six years in the hospital and five in the Emergency Department and the biggest conclusion I can draw is that there must be a better way to help people suffering from mental illness. Mental illness leads to more illness. In August 2021, I worked my last shift as a phlebotomist and, honestly, I don't think I could ever go back.

LISA, Physical Therapist

As a physical therapist, I work with a few post-surgical patients (most are referred to hospital PT places) who, for the most part, want to get off of or never take narcotics because they are scared of them. Their fear is understandable.

A family member recently was heavily pregnant when she developed back spasms. She thought she might be in labor, so she went to the ER. This person (in my opinion) has alcohol substance disorder, but she believes she has it under control. She checked into the ER, and the doctors decided it was not labor, just back spasms. Being close to this family member, she called us from the ER to give us updates. She told us about the discharge instructions including a script for OxyContin. Obviously, in my head, I panicked. I could not fathom how the ER doctor would jump right into prescribing a narcotic for a pregnant woman. And I couldn't help but wonder if anybody at the hospital screened her to see if she had a history of substance abuse.

Luckily, I work with an occupational therapist (OT) who specializes in pregnancy and is just amazing at reducing fear. The occupational therapist called her and her husband for a virtual visit and walked them through what to expect as far as pain. She gave them tips on breathing exercises and physical exercises. She calmly explained how certain medications could affect the baby's development. The good news is that she did not end up using the medication. They were super grateful for the education that was provided by the OT because it really was more fear of the unknown than anything terribly wrong with her back.

A few years ago, I treated a middle-aged woman who had low back pain. She had a somewhat low affect; maybe a little depressed I thought at the time. I did a bunch of work with her in one physical therapy session that included education about what we were then just learning as the neuroscience of pain—meaning that pain is really and truly a response of your body to different stimuli. Our past experiences and behaviors totally modify how we perceive that pain (and it can be made worse or better by what we believe about it). I thought we had a very good session. She left but never came back. I wondered for months what I did wrong because most people at least call in and say they are going to cancel their future appointments; they don't just disappear.

Over a year went by and this woman came into the office one day with flowers and tears in her eyes. She wanted to inform me that she had been in rehab. She told me that the day I explained to her how pain works (and this was not even a good explanation at that point because I was just learning this material) she went home and had no pain. This completely terrified her, because she was dependent on the narcotics she had been taking for years (I don't recall which ones). She spent a week hiding in her house, trying to figure out how she could stay on them. Then, she tried to get off of them on her own and couldn't. Finally, she went to an inpatient rehab (it took her a long time to get to this step because of the stigma surrounding addiction. She didn't want her friends, neighbors, or parents to know what happened). She got clean and wanted to come in and tell me the story.

From my personal and professional perspective, I think where we went wrong (I know there are so many societal reasons and terrible things that the Sackler family and their company did) was to teach people to be scared of pain. We totally taught them the wrong things—like don't move if you have pain, pain means there is tissue damage, etc. Just recently, maybe ten years ago actually, we started to re-teach pain, and I can see the effects of that starting to change things.

TONI, Human Resources Manager

From an employment perspective, many industries have policies and practices to manage substance abuse at work, especially industries that are responsible for public safety, such as schools, transportation, healthcare, etc. For instance, CDL drivers are administered random drug screens, and if they fail, they can't drive. They'll lose their license. They'll lose their source of income; however, we can't afford to put the public at risk either.

Some employees come to work under the influence of alcohol, illegal drugs, or even prescription medications, such as opioids (any medication can be abused) in every industry. It can be one time—maybe someone comes in to work hungover from the night before, or it can be consistent abuse. Some employees don't take their prescribed medication for a mental health diagnosis. In this instance, they may also need to be removed from a workplace environment.

Everybody is so cautious because you don't want to violate the employee's privacy. If employees see someone who is clearly under the influence, they may think that nothing is being done about the issue, but that's not true. We can't share employees' personal information. Employees may choose to think what they want, but human resources won't return to staff and say, "So and so was fired or escorted off the floor because they were high." We wouldn't provide an explanation for the termination to the group. And we wouldn't just write someone up either.

We have to ask what we can do. Can we set them up with a plan to get help? People don't want to discuss these issues, which makes it challenging for us. It is hard to help employees if they don't talk about it or are in denial.

People lose sight of the fact that these are good, everyday people—mothers, fathers, sisters, brothers, husbands, and wives. These people aren't homeless addicts. The truth is that you never really know what someone is managing. And you can't help somebody who doesn't want help. You can try, but ultimately, it is their responsibility—it is their choice.

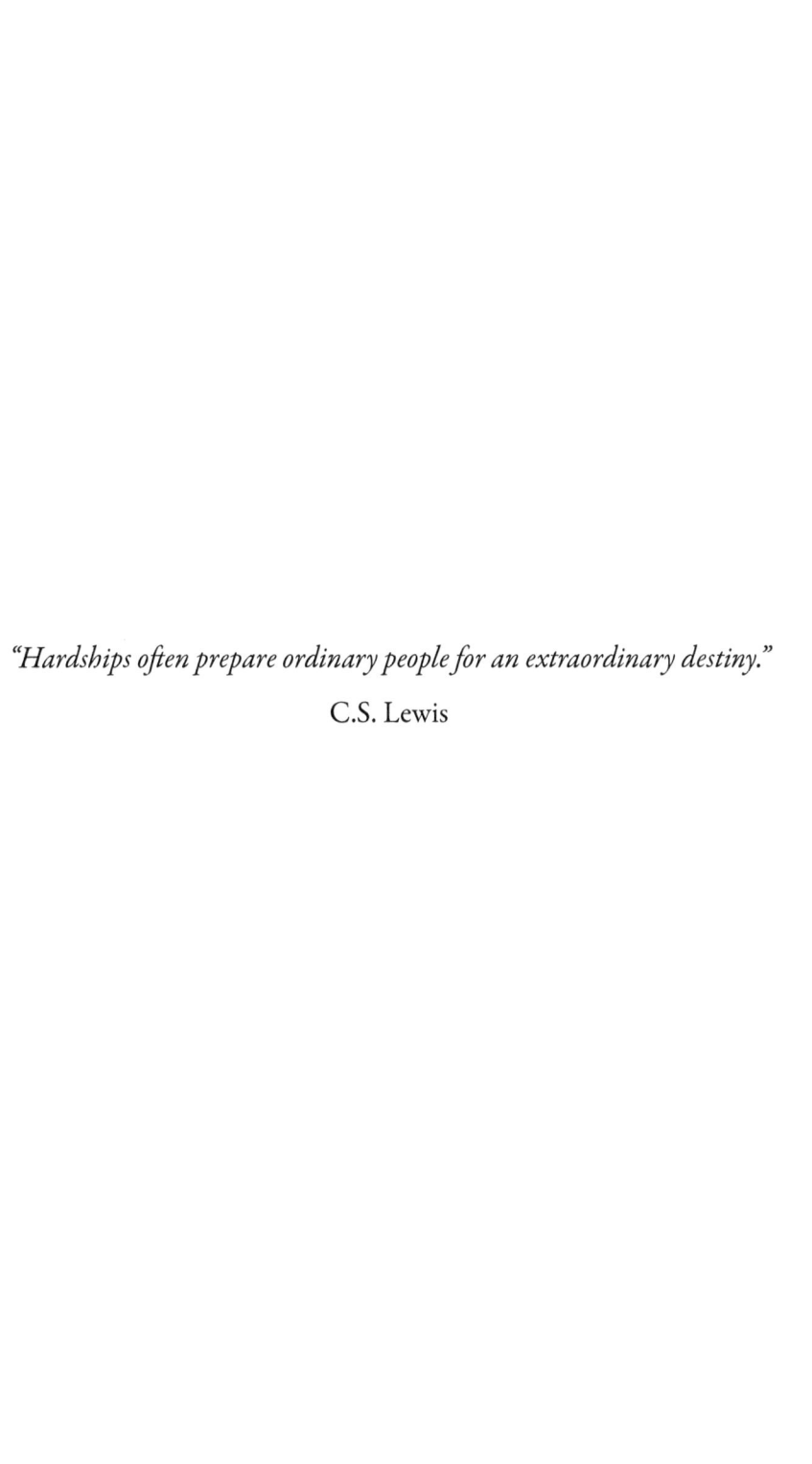

"Hardships often prepare ordinary people for an extraordinary destiny."

C.S. Lewis

CHAPTER NINE

AN UPHILL BATTLE

*By Marly Gaviria
as told to Casey J.*

"FLAKKA? WHAT THE heck is flakka?" I remember asking my fellow nurses. They were just as confused as I was. I have been working as a nurse for well over thirty years (mostly ICU and PCU with a focus in cardiac), but I had no clue what that was. And then about two to three years ago, I learned about the synthetic drug for the first time. Flakka is a form of bath salts, and it makes users violent and mad. It is extremely dangerous and potent.

In our hospital, we had two patients high on the substance. They were able to twist and turn their bodies in ways you couldn't even imagine. One patient's behavior was so out of control, it took seven people to try to calm him down. But the way he was moving prevented us from being able to administer any kind of sedative. He jumped out of bed and started running down the halls like he was flying and disappeared out the front door. We had to call the police because we couldn't catch him.

I believe flakka is also called the cannibal drug because users would eat other people and not even realize what they were doing. I think I remember reading about the police catching someone high on it and eating someone else's nose! Users would run across busy highways, jumping from car to car, naked. Oh, my Lord, there are just so many crazy drugs out there, it's hard to keep track.

When patients come in high on drugs, we do our best to stabilize them. If users have overdosed, they are administered medications to reverse it in the emergency room. We see so many substance abuse cases, and sometimes it seems so hopeless. Our society has turned into "There's nothing we can do." As nurses, we do what we can to help substance abusers, but once the patient walks out the door, it's up to them. We can provide them with information about resources, but we can't force them to go get help. And then one to two weeks later, those same patients show up again with the same issue. They know what they need to do, but they just aren't doing their part. It's up to the person to decide to give up their addiction.

When you're deep in addiction, your body and your mind know they need drugs or alcohol. Substance abusers think, *It makes me feel good. It makes me feel better.* Every time they do it, they think it could be their last but they don't care. They need it too much. So they use, they wake up from their high, and still crave it. The cycle repeats itself over and over again.

We care for a lot of alcoholic patients as well. Some have to be transferred to the ICU and are completely sedated so that we can give their body the proper nutrition it needs. Basically, we put the patient in a coma until the body balances out. Some withdrawals are really bad and must be done correctly. So after a certain number of days, the doctors wake the patient from their comatose state. Even taking such drastic measures to safely enable a patient to withdraw doesn't deter them from using again. Only they can decide to stop. Nobody can do it for them.

I remember when I was just coming in as a nurse at a hospital in New Jersey, I took care of a young girl in her 20s who was an alcoholic. She was a frequent flyer because she would come in once or twice a month. Everybody knew who she was. She had cirrhosis of the liver. We would treat her, discharge her, and then send her on her way. The nurses and I would ask, "Where is her support system? How can we help her?" She didn't get help. All of her organs failed despite the numerous transfusions we gave her. There was nothing else we could do. She died on my watch, and it was the saddest experience I ever had. It's one thing to read about in books, but it's something totally different when tackling a case hands-on.

Over the years, I've become numb to all of it. It still makes me sad, but mostly I'm just very disappointed in the healthcare system. From what I have seen over the years, it is clear the system is broken. Nothing has changed when it comes to helping those suffering from substance use disorder.

Not a single patient has ever been discharged from the hospital straight to rehab. It has to do with insurance—there are a lot of politics involved. Once people are discharged from the hospital, they have to wait and drive themselves to rehab or have someone drive them or they go back to using again. Even if the patient wants to go to rehab, there is no place for us to put them in the hospital in the meantime. They have to leave and go on their own terms. Unfortunately, most patients refuse to go, period, which creates big issues with the families.

We don't have enough rehab centers compared to the number of substance abusers in this country. Our society needs these recovery centers so why doesn't the government put more money toward them? They give money to wars, but why not help more people go to rehab? Some people can get clean on their own, but the majority need assistance, and they just aren't getting it. Our society needs help more than ever, especially with the amount of fentanyl coming in across our borders.

The other day I was watching the news from Colombia because that is where I'm from, and they were discussing fentanyl consumption. And then I watched the news from the United States, and they were talking about their plans to stop Mexico from dispensing fentanyl in our country. Unfortunately, this is all business. The consumers need it and want it, so these suppliers are going to do what they have to do to get consumers what they need. There is a lot of money involved. All of those drugs are making people rich. Not the consumers. Not the families of consumers. We know who's selling it and where it's coming from, but nobody is stopping it. Why? Because of money. Greed is killing people. It's very sad but there is hope.

Some people are sounding the alarm and raising awareness. We need to fight to create a better environment for future generations to grow up in, so we must take action now before it's too late.

Marly Gaviria (photo credit: Marly Gaviria)

"Don't let the past steal your present."

Terri Guillemets

CHAPTER TEN

THE RIPPLE EFFECT OF DRUG USE

By Lynda Wallis

MY MOM–THE WHITE-COLLAR DRUG PEDDLER AND ABUSER

MOM WAS A nurse for a small-town doctor for more than fifteen years. Every week, drug salesmen came to the doctor's office and left bags of prescription drugs as samples for the doctor to hand out to his patients. Every week, Mom came home with white lunch bags filled with drug samples.

Women came from all over to sit at our kitchen table with Mom. They would chat, share stories, laugh, and drink tea. Then Mom would go upstairs to the linen closet to retrieve the samples and would hand white lunch bags to the women—who would leave with eternal gratitude in their hearts and psychic debt to her.

When I was young, I believed in the world I grew up in. I didn't question the authority figures in my life. It never occurred to me until quite recently that it wasn't normal that my mom peddled drugs from the kitchen table. Sounds ludicrous, doesn't it? My mom handed out bags of prescription drugs at our kitchen table, and I didn't see anything wrong with that because she was my mom—a nurse, a respected member of the community, an educated woman, a wife, and a mother. She was even a Cub Scout leader.

During the time Mom was entertaining women at the kitchen table with the promise of free prescription drugs, I smoked pot for the first time. Pot didn't scare me. It was natural, not a man-made chemical from a bottle. I didn't smoke often. The first time I got high, my eyeballs floated above my head, allowing me to view the world from a higher perspective. The flavored wrapping paper left an unexpected taste of strawberries on my lips. It was nice, but I never dared to try anything stronger. Mom didn't seem bothered by my occasional pot smoke or the fact I was dating a much older man in my teenage years. She just didn't seem to care much about me.

After my beloved grandmother (my shero) passed away, my mom and sister became the best of friends—something I was never a part of. Mom never really saw me or acknowledged any of my achievements. She wasn't there for me when I needed her most. On the morning of my first wedding day, she was nowhere to be found. And now my mom is living in a memory care unit, and her brain is slowly erasing everything. I missed so much in my upbringing from the neglect, disinterest, lack of mentorship, and complete lack of any kind of emotional connection with my mom. I paid a heavy price for my naivete.

I left my house at nineteen and sought out men who were terrible for me. You could drop me in a crowded room, and like a moth to a flame, I would make a beeline toward the guy who would be the absolute worst partner for me.

MY LAST MARRIAGE

When I met him, I had been running my own business as an artist/illustrator for about nine years. I was making illustrated signs for nature preserves and earning a solid reputation. The signs I made were beautiful, functional, and informative in a fun way. I also was the in-house mapmaker for a highly regarded regional magazine, *Chicago Wilderness*.

He and I worked together for a few years before developing a personal relationship over our love for nature. We spent hundreds of hours paddling on the waterways and were part of a large team working on an exciting new project called Water Trails in the Chicagoland area. Even though many others had this idea previously, he managed to target the right people in the right agencies with money to back the project.

We wanted to make canoeing and kayaking accessible to people of all skill levels. I was the graphic designer/mapmaker for the new project, and I would have considered him to be the project's spiritual leader. He had amazing charisma and passion for the project and knew how to use both. He was very good, and he was deeply invested in the birth story of Chicago. Everywhere we went, he knew the origin stories and was an excellent storyteller.

After spending so much time with him, in and out of work, I grew to love him very deeply. He loved me too—I think.

During our exhilarating courtship, he was open about his drug use and his love of drugs. He told endless stories, framing his tales as if the bulk of his drug use was behind him. It never occurred to me he would flat-out lie to me about the extent of his current drug use, which he did. I knew he smoked pot regularly, and I wasn't bothered by that initially. I didn't see anything wrong with his drug use because drugs had been normalized in the house I grew up in. I was repeating the cycle and didn't even realize it at the time.

After four years of dating, my children (nine and sixteen) and I took a trip with him and stayed at an eco-resort on St. John, in the U.S. Virgin Islands, for a week. The day of the evening he proposed to me, he disappeared into St. John's hills while my kids and I hung out on the beach. (I later learned it was to drop acid in preparation for asking me to marry him.)

He and I had talked about eventual marriage, but I was in no hurry to marry again, so I was surprised when he asked. I didn't know how to answer. My son filmed his proposal as the four of us sat in our tent as tiny geckos crawled around. In the video, he asked me several times if I would marry him while waving a ring he had secretly bought on our trip into town the day before. My young daughter beamed at us as he proposed.

On the inside, I told myself, "NO, the time isn't right." Eventually, I said, "Yes," and we married a few months later.

MY HUSBAND'S "HEART EVENT" IN MEXICO

Our next big trip was to Mexico. It began with my husband embarking on his search for illegal drugs and alcohol and ended with him in the hospital.

On the way back to the airport, my eleven-year-old daughter and I were in the back seat, enjoying the warm tropical air and the smells we'd come to love in Puerto Vallarta. As our little cab, with its useless shock absorbers, bumped over the charming narrow cobblestone streets, my husband turned to me from the front passenger seat and said with his hand over his heart, "I think I'm having a heart attack. My heart has been pounding wildly since we got up. I don't think I'm going to make it to the airport."

Our cab driver looked at me in the rearview mirror and told me there was a hospital right around the corner. In a moment, he pulled up to a small three-story building in a neighborhood that our American eyes would never have been able to identify as a hospital. The driver helped me escort my husband into the lobby, and he was immediately taken to the ER.

The cab driver sat with my daughter and me in the very small lobby for almost an hour, and his presence calmed me.

Soon, a doctor came out and told us that my husband was **not** having a heart attack. The doctor wanted to admit him to the ICU for a few days while they monitored him as they worked to get his heart rate down to normal and determined the root cause of his dramatic AFib.

My husband, with his nose for illegal drugs, had managed to find a dealer and bought some kind of substance. He also bought illegal moonshine brewed from blue agave plants growing on the side of a mountain. He and I were fairly certain his heart event had been brought on by what he had taken the night before.

His heart rate calmed down after he had been pumped with enough drugs to counteract his racing heart. We met with his doctor, and my husband was forthright about his drug and alcohol use over the past few days as well as his long-term drug use.

The doctor was non-judgmental, cataloged the information, and thanked him for being honest. When the doctor stepped out for a minute, I told my husband I was impressed with his honesty. His response was, "If I don't tell him everything about my drug use, he won't be able to help me."

I was certain my husband was in good hands, safely tucked into the small, but well-equipped ICU. We were told he needed to stay in the hospital for several days and that we would need to stick around for a while so his health could be monitored before he would be declared well enough to fly home.

WITH ENDINGS COME NEW BEGINNINGS

My husband and I did not live together as husband and wife much longer after we returned from Mexico. Disgusted with my husband, my son moved in with his best friend after what should have been a minor disagreement. I was heartbroken, but also relieved he was no longer subjected to my husband's irrational rants and anger.

We lived separately for the last six years of our marriage. Despite the tragic tales, we loved each other and tried to patch up our relationship, but we just couldn't make it work. We made such a mess of our marriage. Both of my children had been badly hurt.

I finally realized how much the marriage was harming me, and the damage was getting worse all the time. Only after that epiphany was I able to move forward and make our divorce happen.

The morning our divorce was to be finalized, after months and months in court, he sent me a voice message telling me he loved me and "not to do this." But I listened to my inner voice—the quiet well of strength I turned to in previous relationships—and followed through. I needed to break free. I've finally gotten to the point today where I can tell myself "Fuck it." I'm completely free and clear of all romantic relationships; it's quite liberating.

Many years have passed since all of this happened, and I am emotionally healthier than ever before in my life. That's not to say that writing this wasn't difficult, because it was. We all suffered from many deep and serious wounds. (Compassionate therapy for all three of us, and the incredible grace of my children have allowed me to forgive myself and heal.) Reflecting on what my kids and I went through has made my choices and actions even more cringe-worthy to me—not because I was a drug user or dealer, but because drug use had been normalized by my mom.

I looked to recreate the dynamic that I saw between my parents—Mom was the Queen, and Dad accepted it. But I knew I didn't want that for my children. Unlike the disrespect I allowed from my partners, I didn't want my children to follow that path. I made certain my children's emotional, social, and intellectual tool belts were overflowing by the time they left home, even if mine wasn't. I made sure to arm them with everything I had been missing. It's served them well. Both are super smart, savvy, and inquisitive with very good boundaries.

A recent photo of Lynda's grown children and Lynda. (photo credit: Lynda Wallis)

TODAY

The price to get where I'm at today has been high—years of broken dreams, devastating heartbreak, and complete scorched-earth endings. But I managed to do well in other areas of my life. I'm an independent businesswoman—successfully running my own business for over three decades. I'm an accomplished artist, and I'm a good mom. I've owned my own home for decades. It was not an easy path, but I did it.

Lynda stands in the Pump House Regional Art Center in LaCrosse, Wisconsin, surrounded by her art. (photo credit: Lynda Wallis)

My life could have taken a much different path given my upbringing and the choices I made. Somehow my belief in myself and my ability to create art has always saved me.

"I don't know where I'm going from here, but I promise it won't be boring."

David Bowie

CHAPTER ELEVEN

IN THE AIR

By Isabelle Vargas

G ROWING UP WITH the desire to "fit in" was always an interesting concept to me. When I was younger (mid-elementary school), "fitting in" was basically having blonde hair and blue eyes. The beginning of middle school was when it became more important. Not only was it about our bodies and relationships, but it was also about what we did. And we would've done anything to fit in and be perceived as "cool." That can be rough for anyone of any age; I'm fifteen now. I still feel a thousand pounds of weight on my shoulders all because of stupid clichés. Why does any of it even matter?

My friends always saw me as the more innocent one—the one who rarely did anything bad. I focused on my goals of wanting to go to New York University and writing. I never got caught up in the crazy things my friends were doing. It was hard for me to make friends as a kid, and it got to the point where I would've done ANYTHING to have a best friend. So, I hung out with people who made me feel like I never belonged anywhere I went—like I was disposable. I was the type to talk about movies that just came out, while they would talk about their weekly hookups. I was muted each time. I mean, of course, everyone would want to hear about the stories of make-outs over my rants about *10 Things I Hate About You*. I felt mortified. But that's not even the worst part.

The worst part was when we all found our "cliques." I saw a lot of my friends change. I saw them turn into somebody they weren't. The "Teenage Dream," they called it. My friends were living in movie scenes but in horrible ways. In a way that left everyone's heads spinning—ways that they could never tell their parents about. Why they really didn't come home that Friday night. Why their eyes were bright red and they were dizzy. I just want to know why they picked drugs and alcohol over experiencing sober teenage lives.

I witnessed so many fade away slowly. They weren't the same people they were five months ago. I mean, yeah, we all change, but did some have to change so drastically? Very few of us stayed the same.

By the end of middle school/beginning of summer, things had grown ten times worse. Of course, during the summer, we all have free time and do reckless things. We craved adrenaline rushes but in different ways. One of mine consisted of trying to do backflips off a diving board. Meanwhile, a girl I knew from school got drunk, became pregnant, and had an abortion. At fourteen, we weren't thinking about having kids of our own; we *were* kids. Of course, we thought about it in the far future, but right now? No way. I even knew people who were addicted to cutting their wrists. It was crazy seeing it all happen—the drinking, the drugs, the self-harm.

It really hit me hard when someone I was close with fell prey to substance abuse. Most people I knew who got caught up in dangerous addictions were predictable, but not him. I saw his normal eyes turn red and painful. He had kind, soft brown eyes before, but then they turned scary, as if something else had taken over. He mumbled. He claimed it was a one-time thing, but one time turned into every night. He tumbled down quickly, and wintertime seemed to only make it worse. I have an idea as to why he turned to smoking and drugs, but I feel the main reason was so he could be "happy." He wanted to fit in. And he started to, but he lost himself in the process.

I don't know if he's still into all of that since we have no contact, but I hope he's okay. Nobody should ever feel that way—like you have to do risky things to "fit in." When you see someone you love go through all of this, it is rough too. It hurts because you feel like you lost control too. I had no idea how to help him. I had no idea how to help anyone, even those I'm close with who deal with their own problems.

This past school year I almost lost a friend to an overdose. It crushed me to think that this beautiful, sweet soul nearly lost her young life to drugs. When the kids at school found out about the overdose and the professional help she was receiving, the awful rumors began to swirl around. Bullying is real and it happens every single day. Teenagers can be cruel. Even my mom can attest to that.

My mom works at a high school, and she has seen a lot during her thirteen years there. She's seen kids go to school high and skip classes, and she's seen kids collapse in the hallways. She just asks herself the question everyone always asks. *Why?*

It is true that many kids engage in bad habits, but not all of us cave into peer pressure. Some of us just want to enjoy our teenage years sober. Some of us manage to find healthier alternatives to drinking, drugs, or self-harm. For me and my friend, music is our passion. We find solace in it. Music always takes me to some type of other—kind of feels like I'm floating, and nothing else matters. With music, I can scream, laugh, cry, jump, and dance. It's an escape—an escape from the horrible world and reality. The lyrics run through my brain, and I can always relate, and it makes me feel safe. Music has saved my life so many times. It's literally the air I breathe. From blasting Paramore or Greta Van Fleet to crying to Conan Gray, then somehow screaming to Taylor Swift and Harry Styles, it is how I live. And I can never be mad about it. I am grateful I do not suffer from any harmful addictions.

Addiction is hard. It's a labyrinth. You feel like no matter which path you take, there's no real exit. Real David Bowie moment. Nobody should have to lose their lives or lose someone at all to a substance. People believe these substances are good for them, but they're not. They just cause more problems. We all have our pain, but we must choose to leave it behind in order to move forward. Everyone has their own story (whether or not they decide to share it), and it is our job to learn and grow from the experiences.

The day I was able to breathe–Harry Styles concert. (photo credit: Isabelle Vargas)

*"Our greatest glory is not in never failing,
but in rising up every time we fail."*

Confucius

PART TWO
RECOVERY & ACTIVISM

"Recovery is an ongoing process, for both the addict and his or her family. In recovery, there is hope. And hope is a wonderful thing."

Dean Dauphinais

CHAPTER TWELVE

RECOVERY IS POSSIBLE

By Tony Campolo LPC, LCADC, DBTC, CCTP, ACS
as told to Casey J.

THE LAST DAY I used any substances was on September 16, 1987. I was arrested on the lower east side of Manhattan with a large amount of heroin and cocaine along with several syringes. I got clean in New York City. I remain active in a 12-step recovery program that addresses the disease of addiction. I have maintained complete and total abstinence since September 17, 1987.

My friends in the program call me "Tony Shoes." At that time, there were many Tonys in the program, so what you did for a living (I worked in the shoe industry) became like a nickname.

I grew up in a very Italian family. I was born in Brooklyn, New York, and eventually moved to Staten Island, New York. Wine was a big part of my culture. While growing up, it was not uncommon for us to have a little wine in our soda; however, I liked it too much and put soda in my wine. I was exposed to cannabis around this time. Basically, I was introduced to different substances (legal and illegal) at a very early age.

My mother and sister were taking prescription amphetamine-based diet pills (yellow jackets). I started stealing them, along with opiate-based pain medications that were prescribed to my father after his injury. Shortly after, I began experimenting with heroin and cocaine.

My mother was diagnosed with cancer when I was twelve. Sadly, it spread throughout her body, and she passed away when I was sixteen years old. She was only forty-two years old at the time of her death. Focusing on school was very difficult for me after she passed. I cut school often and barely attended any classes. I believe the school only passed me because they felt sorry for me and my situation. I would show up high all the time on cannabis, Quaaludes, and alcohol. This is when my drug use really escalated. I was very active in martial arts. But after my mother passed, my addiction progressed to daily use, and I walked away from years of training.

I'm not going to go into detail, but I suffered from a significant amount of trauma in my childhood. I saw and heard things I shouldn't have, and it really impacted my life. Feelings were not openly discussed in my family. My dad was very blue collar—a New York City fireman, first generation, Italian American from Brooklyn. I believe my dad did the best he could at the time with what he knew, but he didn't handle my mother's death well either. Often, I would be leaving for school in the morning, and he would be walking in the door after being out all night drinking and trying to pick up women.

I was re-introduced to heroin by a musician I knew. I would attend band practice with him and along the way, they would stop and buy drugs. I asked to try heroin. Initially, they said no, but eventually, they let me snort it. A short time later, I began using intravenously (IV). In the late '70s-early '80s, I became very much involved in the punk rock scene in New York City and found a group of people who were using as well. I fit right in with the lifestyle they were living.

I lied, stole, cheated, and manipulated others to maintain my habit. I was in countless detoxes and several therapeutic communities. I would not use for brief periods, relapse, and then seek treatment once again. I lied my way through all of it. I was on and off methadone (two clinics at the same time). However, I was still using large amounts of other drugs (cocaine, pills, alcohol, cannabis, etc.).

My experience withdrawing from methadone was much worse than heroin. I used large amounts of heroin to wean myself off methadone. I honestly did not have a positive experience with opiate-replacement treatments.

I must have been around twenty-one years old when I completed yet another therapeutic community and did not use for a few years. Even though I was no longer using drugs, I continued doing everything an addict does—I lied, conned, manipulated, and cheated. I was self-centered, angry, and full of shame and guilt. I really didn't like who I was as a person.

I married my first wife when I was around twenty-three years old. We were together for almost two years before she got sick. Our eldest son was born around this time too. This was in the 1980s. I thought she had HIV (Human Immunodeficiency Virus), and I thought she gave it to our son. I thought it was all my fault for using needles. I believed I had the virus and then I passed it on to her and our child. Two of my ex-girlfriends died from HIV along with many friends I shared needles with, so I was really paranoid and angry with myself. Somehow, I was spared and didn't contract HIV. I guess God had other plans for me.

Shortly after, I was diagnosed with non-A, non-B Hepatitis (which is now called Hepatitis C). The virus was new and not much was known about it. Doctors gave me two years to live. I took time off work to help my sick wife and infant son. I wound up losing my job. I was beginning to feel hopeless.

I went job hunting in Manhattan daily and was not getting any leads. My anxiety was obvious while being interviewed. I had the not-so-bright idea to take a cab to the lower east side of Manhattan, which was like a supermarket for drugs during this time. Forty to fifty people would wait in line on the streets to buy drugs. Sometimes, I would wait for people to buy drugs, and then I would rob them—stealing the drugs and any money they had. I was caught up in the grip of full-blown addiction. Even after four years of not using, my addiction still lived inside of me. This was the day I got arrested, and it was the last day I used. I was twenty-five years old at the time.

I was placed in a holding cell in lower Manhattan with a homeless Australian crack addict. I looked at this man and thought to myself *you are really messed up.* Then reality hit me—*I'm in the same cell as him.* While in the holding cell, two women walked by with helpline cards that read "If you're sick and tired of being sick and tired, give us a call." It was the helpline number for what would be my future fellowship in New York City.

I was allowed my one phone call and called my wife. She told me not to come home. They ran my name and found an outstanding warrant in Brooklyn from years ago, so I got stuck in the system for a few days. I was brought back and forth between Manhattan and Brooklyn to stand before judges. Thank God it was the '80s, and I was released with some fines in both boroughs. As long as I remained out of trouble for a few years, these charges would eventually disappear from my record.

I was able to negotiate with my wife to let me stay in a vacant store-front that her father owned and was converting into an apartment until I found treatment. I called many different facilities, and all had year-long waiting lists. I had no insurance and kept getting directed to attend 12-step recovery which focused on addiction. I called up a psychiatrist and demanded to speak to him. At first, they refused. I ended up making some demands with some threats (not proud of this), and soon enough, the doctor was on the other end of the line. Again, I was directed to the same fellowship. His exact words were, "I'm not going to tell you that you don't have any mental health problems, but you need to get clean first. Did you ever hear of the 12-step fellowship?" I was receiving the same message from everywhere. I called the helpline number from the card I was given in the holding cell and found out where the closest meeting was to where I was living.

When I walked into my first meeting, the first guy I recognized was a man whose car I had jumped out of years before. The guy was so high, I felt I had better chances of surviving by jumping out of a moving vehicle than staying with him. His dad was a big shot for the New York City police, so we were usually left alone if we got pulled over and had drugs in our possession.

I started watching this one guy at the meetings. He seemed to know what he was talking about, so I asked him to sponsor me. He told me to ask for phone numbers at every meeting I went to during my first ninety days, so I would have ninety numbers by the end of ninety days. I ended up with over 150 numbers and attended nearly 600 meetings in my first year. He became my first sponsor at that meeting.

I was unaware of this at the time, but he was one of the first people in New York City diagnosed with HIV (remember that at this time I still thought I had the virus). He went with me to clinics to get tested numerous times. I tested negative each time. Back then, we did not know much about this disease, so I needed to make sure. I didn't want to risk infecting my family.

Just shy of my fourth year clean, my family and I followed my father-in-law's business and moved to Pennsylvania. The cost of living was cheaper, and I wanted a better life for my family. I continued attending meetings and remained connected to the fellowship.

Years later, I discovered my wife was having an affair. So, after eighteen years together, we divorced. This was a very difficult time for me. I surrounded myself with recovering individuals. I was committed to not using "no matter what." What I recognized through doing extensive work on myself was that even though she had the affair (which was wrong), I had emotionally checked out of the marriage years before.

A few years later, I met my second wife, and we had a son together. Unfortunately, this was a big mistake (the marriage, not my son). After a few years, we separated and then divorced. I was eventually awarded sole legal and primary physical custody of my son. This is something I would never have been able to do if I was still using.

During this time, I was diagnosed with Lymphoma. I endured several rounds of chemotherapy, and I'm happy to say to this day I remain cancer free.

In the 1990s, I returned to school and completed an eighteen-credit Addictions Studies Program, and I received my first-ever A. I remember the professor told his story about addiction and recovery. It motivated me and gave me hope that addicts can and do recover.

I started working as a counselor in a detox unit and obtained my Certified Addiction Counselor credential at that time. While I did well, I didn't like the idea that I was being supervised by people with less knowledge than me but who had received more education and degrees. I decided to return to school and earned my bachelor's degree in psychology. I was never a big fan of school and never had intentions of going this far, never mind even further.

A few years later, after working several other jobs as an addiction therapist, I began working in a private, long-term rehabilitation facility in New Jersey that treats those struggling with substance use and co-occurring mental health disorders. Times were changing, and I was told I needed to obtain my master's degree and licensure. If I didn't, I would be forced to change my position and take a significant pay cut. It took me eighteen months to complete a sixty-credit master's degree clinical program in counseling (which was crazy to do in such a short period of time). After several years of supervision, I had my LPC (Licensed Professional Counselor) in Pennsylvania, and my LCADC (Licensed Clinical Alcohol and Drug Counselor) in New Jersey. Additionally, I hold credentials in trauma, dialectical behavioral therapy, anger, gambling, co-occurring disorders, and clinical supervision.

I started a small private practice in Bethlehem, Pennsylvania, where I treat patients with both mental health and substance use disorders. I also provide a supervision group for post-master's degree individuals working toward clinical licensure.

Due to some of the custody issues, the judge wanted me to work in Pennsylvania, feeling it would be better if I was closer to home.

I obtained a clinical supervisor position for a privately owned facility. Unfortunately, it was sold to a large behavioral health corporation that seemed to be less focused on clients and more focused on numbers. While I understand business is business, I highly value quality patient care. When this change occurred, I did not feel the program was run ethically, and I no longer felt comfortable working there. I decided to expand my private practice while searching for a second source of income.

I decided to apply as a fee-for-service independent contractor at a brain injury rehab. Once the interviewer became aware of my personal and professional background, I was informed that a high percentage of their patients had past histories of substance use. Later on, through research, I became aware of the high correlation between traumatic brain injury and substance abuse.

For me, complete and total abstinence is the only thing that has ever worked, along with committing to the 12-step recovery program. What I've learned over the years is that addiction is a shapeshifter. If you don't maintain your recovery, there is a very real chance of returning to use, regardless of your clean time or switching to other maladaptive behaviors. I believe drugs are what you put into your body; addiction is the funny-looking thing between your ears.

I have known many addicts who have died from this disease, but I also know a lot of addicts who have stayed clean for decades. Recovery is possible. Anybody who believes addicts can't recover, couldn't be more wrong. I have seen countless addicts become very successful in their lives after they get clean. Miracles do happen; I see them every day.

If you are reading this and are suffering from the disease of addiction, know that help is available. The lie is dead—addicts can and do recover. I am living proof that we don't have to use no matter what happens in our lives.

I would like to close with one of my favorite quotes:

"In the beginner's mind there are many possibilities, but in the expert's there are few."

Shunryu Suzuki, *Zen Mind, Beginner's Mind: Informal Talks on Zen Meditation and Practice*

Much Love and Respect to you all, Tony
https://www.campolocounseling.com/

"These feelings, no matter how painful, are part of living. Today, we are alive—not anesthetized, not sedated, not passed out. Take control of your feelings and through action you can change. Today, as every day of sober living, we have a choice."

Ann D. Clark

CHAPTER THIRTEEN

HOLISTIC MODALITIES
FOR RECOVERY

By Ryan Elizabeth McLaughlin, LAc, MSOM
https://www.flourishoflifemedicine.com/

ADDICTION. A SINGLE word that brings up so many thoughts and emotions, judgments, and grief. A label and concept that feels so misunderstood. I hold the perspective that addiction is repeated action coming from an internal impulse of the body and nervous system trying to self-regulate. The greatest thing we can do to support people experiencing addictive patterns is lean in—offer support through nervous system regulation. Addiction is the body's attempt to regulate it.

Acupuncture is a modality that provides nervous system regulation through the physical contact of ultra-fine needles with various points throughout the body. The ancient science of East Asian medicine provides us with tools to bring the body back into homeostasis, back into regulation. The modalities of acupuncture, breathwork, qi gong, dietary support, and herbal medicine can be combined to provide a profound impact on the inner terrain of the individual. When an individual is supported from the inside out and the outside in, a place of stillness can be found in the body. The body has less desire to find stillness or regulation externally, i.e. substance use, social media scrolling, etc. People begin to learn that being still can be a safe experience; one of satisfaction and rejuvenation.

During my final years of Chinese Medicine school, I was given the opportunity to intern off-site at a recovery support model in Portland, Oregon, called Central City Concern. Among the plethora of health and social support services they provided to community members needing support, all individuals currently active in their recovery process had access to free unlimited acupuncture in a group setting. During my weekly shifts there, I came into contact with the most courageous individuals who were filled with curiosity and gratitude for acupuncture. Individuals could choose to come into the acupuncture clinic multiple times a day if they were looking for support. During their sessions there, people felt seen. People felt cared for. They knew they had a community rooting for them, which was there to teach them tangible methods of regulating their nervous systems.

Another model of acupuncture support during recovery of historical significance involved the Black Panthers in 1970. The Bronx, New York, community members were determined to radically support the addiction recovery process while witnessing long lines at methadone clinics and people on the streets dying of heroin overdoses. They were sick of social injustice, lack of medical care, and lack of resources. Desperate for other alternatives to freedom, and away from the addictive methadone treatments, Lincoln Detox hired Mutulu Shakur as director of education. He had his team trained in acupuncture and then started the Lincoln Detox acupuncture training program. As more people learned to perform acupuncture in a detox setting, more community members were supported. Shakur and the Black Panthers brought acupuncture into the forefront as a method of treating people with addiction.

The community model of acupuncture supporting addiction recovery should be available everywhere. We are in a crisis of nervous system regulation in the United States. People are consuming tainted substances, prescribed substances, toxic food substances, and massive amounts of auditory and electronic information every minute of every day. As a nation and a world of humans constantly looking to the next thing for stimulation/release, we need to have access to tools for nervous system regulation and holistic support. There are simple ways we can support ourselves and be supported—eating healthy foods and addressing the gut microbiome, reducing toxic loads in our bodies, learning to breathe fully and calm our minds, and finding moments of gratitude, movement, and access to acupuncture.

Addiction behavior and mindset have a way of weaving themselves into everyone's lives in one form or another, whether someone is identifying with it or not. I have personally taken the steps to break the cycle of addiction in my own family, though not a single member would self-identify as an alcoholic. I got to watch as certain friends and family members interacted with me differently, or stopped calling me altogether, but I knew it was because my choices were creating an opportunity for them to question their own indulgences, and that made people uncomfortable. It takes courage to question your own actions, and that is why I am so inspired by the people I have met in recovery settings. Recovery takes courage.

I have mourned the lives of friends gone too soon from overdoses—accidental or not. I look around in this world at the celebration and expectation of overindulgence, unless that fine line is crossed, and honestly, it brings up sadness. And then, knowing modalities exist that could be of great benefit and are not always accessible to those who need them, brings up anger. And anger, anger is powerful. I like to reframe anger as an unstoppable force for action. And that—that is a force to be reckoned with.

After all, aren't we all recovering from something?

Ryan soaking in the warm rays in Puerto Rico.
(photo credit: Ryan Elizabeth McLaughlin, February 11, 2022)

"If you hear a voice within you say 'you cannot paint,' then by all means paint and that voice will be silenced."

Vincent Van Gogh

CHAPTER FOURTEEN

SPEAKING UP FOR BEN

BREAK THE SILENCE—END THE STIGMA—NEVER FORGET

*By Rhonda Miller, Certified Family Recovery Specialist,
Certified Grief Educator*

BEAUTIFUL BOY

MY BEAUTIFUL BOY, Benjamin Alden Miller, entered this world in the wee hours of Saturday, August 8, 1992, in sunny San Jose, California, weighing in at a healthy seven pounds, seven ounces. His birth experience was peaceful and joyous. Baby Ben was beautiful, precious, and perfect.

On the outside, Ben looked like he had it all: intelligence, humorous wit, athletic ability, musical talent—complete with piercing blue eyes, and a famously thick mop of hair. He had an impish grin with a dimpled chin that could steal any heart. Ben was insightful and possessed the innate ability to connect and forge a relationship with anyone he met—regardless of their background or socioeconomic status. Ben described himself as "determined...when I set my mind to accomplish something, I work very hard to achieve it." Charismatic and charming—yet inwardly, Ben was sensitive and insecure and struggled with a lack of self-esteem and self-confidence for many years. We were devoted to helping Ben grow into a healthy young man and giving him guidance and all the love in our hearts, but we learned in time that our love was not enough to shield him from the evils in the world.

When Ben was young, he loved playing soccer. This was a tremendously positive experience, where his self-confidence grew and strong friendships formed. But during the summer of 2005, I noticed that Ben became more isolated. He spent much of his time on the computer and limited time interacting in person with other kids. As he grew older, he missed a lot of school. I brought this to the attention of the assistant principal, and he had a discussion with Ben, but that was the extent of it. Looking back, these were early symptoms of Ben's depression.

WHAT HAPPENED TO MY SON?

By the spring of 2008, our happy 15-year-old son had begun exhibiting alarming signs of underlying problems. I brought Ben to see his pediatrician to address his anxiety and possible depression issues, but my concerns were dismissed, and no clinical follow-up was recommended.

That fall Ben's personality changed. He began exhibiting angry and aggressive behavior. Using hostility and profanity, he refused to respect family rules. One night when his father was away on business and I was sleeping, Ben stormed into my bedroom belligerently. Terrified, I cried, "Who are you and what have you done with my son?" He growled, "Your son is gone, and he is not coming back!" I was alarmed. In time, it would prove a prophetic utterance.

By the following spring, Ben was diagnosed with oppositional defiant disorder and underwent neuropsychological testing. Shortly afterward, Ben started complaining of severe headaches, so he was referred to an allergist to be tested. No significant allergies were detected, but the allergist's discharge paperwork stated migraines could also be experienced from hangovers. We continued to turn over every rock looking for answers. No one seemed to be able to get to the bottom of Ben's inability to get out of bed in the morning. "Too much screen time before bed...too much Red Bull consumption at night...too much loud music...too much sugary food." These were the responses from the medical community.

THE DOWNWARD SPIRAL

To the best of my ability, I searched for answers and found them on the internet. The signs were there—all the earmarks of substance use. While my husband was not overly concerned and believed it to be typical teenage experimentation (as is often the case), I feared it could be more—especially given the family history of substance abuse. Ben had been exhibiting many of the signs of drug use—including a change in personality, change in friends, change in appearance, truancy, and dropping grades. We continued meeting weekly with our family therapist for two-hour sessions. We were guided in creating the first of many behavioral contracts with Ben.

After a disturbing incident at one of his friend's houses, we rushed Ben to the emergency room, where they performed a psychiatric evaluation and took blood and urine samples. During the intake, Ben admitted that he had been depressed for months and began taking Adderall at the end of June. He admitted to abusing the club drug, Ecstasy, laced with heroin, coke, and meth, the previous two weeks. He became increasingly depressed when he stopped the Ecstasy, so he self-medicated by crushing and snorting Adderall. His urine screen showed marijuana. He admitted drinking alcohol for the first time at age fifteen (though I doubt this) and stated that during the summer he drank ten to fifteen times per month, twelve cans of beer or shots at a time.

The ER visit resulted in Ben receiving a referral for an evaluation at the hospital's adolescent behavioral health unit. The director, seemingly sincere, told Ben he did believe that he was struggling with mental health issues—but they could not help him until he got his drug addiction under control for twelve months! Are you kidding? Ben was self-medicating to quell his mental health issues, which resulted in an addiction. However, the director was adamant and refused to treat him.

After contacting our insurance company, Ben's pediatrician, and numerous addiction outpatient facilities, I finally located an intensive outpatient program for adolescents. By late July 2009, Ben was accepted into the program. While I believe Ben earnestly wanted to fight his disease, he quickly learned from his peers in treatment how to work the system—and they were not serious about recovery. This was the beginning of a long journey through many inpatient rehabs to help our very ill son.

At our insistence, Ben went to Narcotics Anonymous meetings and began working with a sponsor but didn't follow through. He wanted to be a "normal" kid. He underestimated the power of his addiction. He promised himself he would never go back to inpatient. And over the next few years, when given an ultimatum because he continuously lied, stole from us, and violated our boundaries, rather than go back into inpatient treatment, Ben would choose to leave our home.

SUBOXONE TO THE RESCUE?

Ben sought to recover from his opioid addiction with the aid of Suboxone. Costing $100/month out-of-pocket, there was no way Ben could have afforded to pay for this on his own. We would do nearly anything to help our son get the help he needed; we gladly paid. He was having great difficulty managing the opioid cravings, so I contacted a psychiatric practice that specialized in addiction treatment and pleaded for Ben to be seen. Once they learned that Ben was on Suboxone, he was denied treatment. They would not see Ben until he was off all drugs.

I attended Ben's monthly appointments with his primary physician who prescribed him Suboxone. At his initial appointment, the physician informed me that he would gradually taper Ben off it. However, the doctor continued to prescribe and didn't explain his reduction strategy. I watched Ben struggle and physically and spiritually wither away. I finally told the doctor that Ben needed to get off Suboxone so that he could receive inpatient drug addiction treatment.

BLOCKED ACCESS TO MEDICATION FOR OPIOID USE DISORDER (MOUD)

The doctor ordered a urine drug screen. Once the doctor discovered Ben had traces of marijuana and cocaine in his system, he abruptly dismissed him as a patient and cut off Ben's Suboxone treatment—cold turkey. In withdrawal, Ben returned to opioids.

We admitted Ben to an inpatient facility for the third time. We instructed his counselor to find a sober living home Ben could be discharged to—that he could not return to our home. Against our directive, after only nine days of treatment, on a rainy Saturday night at 5 p.m., a facility van pulled up to our house and dropped Ben and his bag on our doorstep. Our sick son was clean and vulnerable; of course, we gave him shelter, but that didn't last long. Ben consistently broke our house rules, forcing us to kick him out. Ben became homeless. After a time, he was motivated to find housing and secured a job. But the pattern soon repeated itself; Ben lost his job, bounced checks, and received an eviction notice.

In February 2015, Ben became so desperate that he broke into our house, stole electronics, and forged three checks. We called the police and filed a report. An investigation was completed. Enough evidence was collected to arrest Ben on felony charges. We were hoping to use this as leverage to get him to agree to treatment. After many years of resistance, he finally agreed to go back into rehab. I called our insurance provider and was on the phone with them and the rehab for most of the day. The representative kept throwing up roadblocks to approve Ben for treatment, until I cried, "My child is dying, please help us!" and Ben also got on the phone, pleading for help. Eventually, a rehab facility took him in.

During the years of his addiction, Ben was admitted to inpatient rehab a total of eleven times. The first nine rehabs did not offer him medication for opioid use disorder, even though he had a severe opioid use disorder. It wasn't until his 10th rehab stint that he was offered Vivitrol. Insurance often cut off coverage during his inpatient treatment, resulting in Ben's premature discharge. When it was time for Ben's monthly Vivitrol shot, the physician was on vacation with no on-call doctor authorized to administer it. It was an incredibly stressful time for me.

My son's substance use disorder had nearly killed me. The emotional stress, chaos, and turmoil had taken a tremendous toll on my health. In constant fear, I watched my son spiral downward. I became so desperate I proactively sought help in a variety of support meetings and counseling.

SAYING GOODBYE

On July 24, 2016, Ben visited with us before my husband and I left for Europe for our 30th-anniversary celebration—a trip we had planned for years. I was very nervous to leave, but my recovery program taught me that I must practice self-care and focus on myself—to live my life. Minutes before we departed, I recorded a video on my iPhone, the last conversation I had with Ben. Sitting on the couch in our family room, next to each other; I had my beautiful boy back. He was tender and sweet, felt proud of himself, and had hope for the future. So did I.

After a week in Paris, my husband and I landed in Prague, Czech Republic, on July 31, 2016. We had plans to go out for dinner and a classical concert, but I felt sick. I had the strangest pain in my stomach, nothing like I had ever experienced before. We were texting Ben, letting him know we had arrived safely. We had a nice exchange; he was happy and getting situated in the new apartment he had moved into the night before.

Little did we know that hours later, Ben drove to the Philadelphia area to procure heroin to satisfy his intense cravings. He returned to his apartment after 11:30 p.m., where his roommate was watching television. Ben locked himself in the shared bathroom and turned on the shower. After some time, his roommate decided to check on him. No answer.

In the wee hours after midnight, his roommate busted down the bathroom door. He found Ben, fatally poisoned by 100% fentanyl. Ben died on August 1, 2016—one week before his 24th birthday.

FINDING MY ANGER, FINDING MY VOICE

When Ben died, a large part of me died too. I descended into a deep depression and was not very functional for several years. Two years into my grief, I was invited to join other bereaved families in a protest march at Purdue Pharmaceutical headquarters in Stamford, Connecticut. I found inner strength by getting in touch with my anger and became an advocate. I joined hundreds of bereaved families protesting the Sackler family's role in creating this public health crisis by aggressively marketing OxyContin as non-addictive, fueling the overdose epidemic. And every year, on August 31st, we join a Fed Up! Rally in honor of those who lost their lives to substance use disorder.

SPEAKING UP FOR BEN

In September 2018, my family and I decided to take action. We founded a 501(c)3 nonprofit corporation, Speak Up for BEN, Inc. Our surviving son named the corporation and created a tagline from an acronym of Ben's name: Break the silence, End the stigma, Never forget. Our mission is "Through compassion and understanding of the family disease of addiction, we seek to provide education, support, comfort, and healing to people who are at risk for, experiencing, or recovering from substance use disorder, their families, and the families of those who lost their battle."

Shortly after that, we were awarded a contract from Northampton County Drug and Alcohol Division to open the OASIS Community Center. This is the first recovery center in the Commonwealth of Pennsylvania for families and friends impacted by a loved one's substance use—perhaps in the nation. I spoke on behalf of all families, like ours, who had nowhere to turn to for help and no idea how to find resources. My priority in establishing programs was to create support for families grieving a loss from a substance-related death. Death by addiction carries such a strong stigma; we falsely carry shame and blame and often remain in isolation as a result. Our grief is typically overlooked, minimized, and disenfranchised—and sadly, often even in traditional grief groups. This complicated grief can be overwhelming.

I work with families every day and, drawing from my experience, strength, and hope, guide them to resources in our community and at our center. We began by offering nine support groups, including all the groups that helped me, as well as a full calendar of holistic, healing activities. We also offer a professionally facilitated grief support group and a family counseling group. To enhance my qualifications, in 2019, I was credentialed by the Commonwealth of Pennsylvania as a Certified Family Recovery Specialist (CFRS) and later received credentialing as a Certified Grief Educator.

LIVING IN THIS NEW NORMAL, ONE DAY AT A TIME

I cannot describe the immense pain I carry...day in, day out...year after year...for not being able to save my son. Looking back, there seem to be so many gaps and system failures. He should have been able to access the lifesaving Vivitrol injection within the timeframe he needed it. My family and I are now speaking up to prevent other tragedies like our family has known. For example, had more physicians been able to prescribe Vivitrol, Ben would have had a chance.

Losing my son has been the most devastating experience of my life. And, to make it so much more painful, I grieved without the support of family and most friends. My family of origin and my husband's family of origin all abandoned us when our son died. The dysfunctional relationships had already been strained, but Ben's death ended them. Neighbors and friends also left us. The disease of addiction and the stigma associated with it often breaks down relationships.

I will never ever get over losing my precious son, Ben. I will grieve forever. I will spend the rest of my life striving to experience a measure of healing, one day at a time. And I hope I can help other bereaved families find a bit of peace. 'Til we meet our loved ones again.

This is my story. I hope it will somehow be of help to others in a meaningful way. Below, I included the letter I wrote and read to my son on April 8, 2015, just before he was discharged from the inpatient facility. My husband and I were asked to write to Ben, explaining how his addiction impacted us.

Peace,
Rhonda
Ben's Mom

SpeakUpForBen.org | OasisBethlehem.org

MY IMPACT LETTER:

Dear Ben,

I am so thankful that you are in treatment and that you desire to get well and choose life. I believe, beyond a shadow of a doubt, that God brought you to this rehab and has cleared a pathway for you to grow in sustained recovery through sober support put in place in Florida. So many doors have miraculously opened for you; clearly, the hand of God is at work in your life—guiding you on the pathway to health and wholeness, and serenity.

I love you more than I can express in words. I love you for what you have been and for what I know you can be. I have so many wonderful memories of you while you were growing up. From the moment you were conceived, I prayed for you and cared for you. The day that you were born was the most joyful day of my life; we had a beautiful delivery experience—I refused all pain medications, as I wanted your birth to be completely free of the influence of drugs. I was completely smitten by you and fell deeply in love with that precious baby boy. I have continuously asked for God's guidance to help me be the mom you need. I have prayed for you every single day of your life—you are God's gift to me.

I loved being at home with you, playing with you, doing everything, and going everywhere together. I loved singing songs with you, coloring and building Legos with you, and reading stories to you. I loved decorating Easter eggs with you, picking out pumpkins, building gingerbread houses together, and decorating our Christmas tree. I loved being your Sunday School teacher, along with Dad. I loved always being home when you got off the bus from school, waiting for you with freshly baked banana muffins and a warm smile and hug. I loved helping you with homework and creating special school projects together. I loved being your "room mom" at school and attending all of your field trips and school parties and programs right alongside you. I loved taking you to sports practices and guitar lessons. I loved attending your basketball and baseball games, soccer tournaments, and swim meets, always cheering you on. I loved arranging your get-togethers with friends and hosting birthday parties for you. I loved watching you grow into a confident, accomplished young man, so full of promise.

You were always so happy and joyful, funny, and bright—you always brought a smile to my face and made me laugh! I loved hearing you sing, and I loved seeing your creativity flourish in music and photography. I miss our times hanging out together and our talks. I really miss you being an engaged member of our family. I miss you coming with our family on vacations, and spending holidays with us. I miss you being around us, enjoying each other's company at family dinners, movies, and outings—and just hanging out at home with us, being a part of us, your family.

When you began abusing drugs, you left us. You no longer wanted to engage with us. You no longer wanted to be an active part of our family; you stopped attending most family functions. I watched, with pain, as you abandoned your dreams—you had a rising and promising soccer career that you had worked very hard to achieve, and you abandoned your honorable academic career. As drugs became your sole focus, you ceased participating in life. When I looked into your eyes, I saw a withered, shallow, empty soul. A shell, without life. You were gone.

The past seven years have been a very dark and painful chapter of my life. After dragging you to the ER when you went missing for three days in the summer of 2009, the reality of the excruciating journey ahead was too much for me to accept. However, the signs were ever before me, as I helplessly watched you spiral down—car accidents; dozens of unpaid tickets and fines; warrants for your arrest; lost jobs; evictions. Coin collections were stolen, credit cards abused, bounced checks, electronics, and money stolen. The chronic and elaborate lies. Manipulation of everyone around you—but most destructive was pitting your dad and me against each other. You stole our cars in search of drugs. I watched you lose everything you owned—your car, your license, your Apple computers, numerous iPhones, your apartment full of furnishings, a beautiful wardrobe, your good friends, your beautiful photography, and all of the amazing music you worked so diligently to create.

I watched you neglect every aspect of caring for yourself; you became homeless, ultimately living in a shelter, and almost lost most of your teeth as they were rotting from neglect. I put you in rehab three times previous to this one, but it was always *me* desperately trying to *help* you when only you can help yourself. The anxiety I experienced was alarming. I made myself crazy trying to hide things from you. I didn't feel safe in my own home—I locked my bedroom door when alone with you at night, and we invested in four safes to protect our valuables; still, we never could keep everything from your theft. In what I believe was your desperate cry for help, our house was broken into, more electronics and my last digital camera were stolen, and checks were forged. As you hit bottom, recklessness exposed the severity of the state you were in. This was the most catastrophic of your crisis. The distressing, pathetic state you were in was devastating to witness and horrific to experience.

It breaks my heart to have seen you so ill over the last seven years, and it breaks my heart to see you through the eyes of others who care. This horrible disease called addiction has robbed you and our family of joy and life and has sapped most of our strength as well as our health.

I, too, became ill. I became bedridden with despair as I watched my dreams for your life slip away. I suffered major depression as I agonized; so utterly helpless, I watched you deteriorate, dying before my eyes. Our family became sick as we desperately tried to save you. Your dad and I abandoned ourselves—and each other—as we frantically did everything we thought to do to halt you from destroying yourself. In the process, we died spiritually, and so did our marriage. I neglected everyone and everything around me as I anxiously focused all of my energy in desperate attempts to stop you from killing yourself. And in doing so, it nearly killed me.

Now, I must choose to live. I must let you go and give you back to God. By releasing you with love, I give you the dignity to live the life you choose. Ben, I am so proud of the steps you have taken to get help and begin your recovery. Your willingness to leave everything and everyone behind and relocate to a recovering community gives me hope. By changing your people, places, and things—by deleting Facebook and your iCloud, by changing your phone number and email address, you are cleaning the slate, and positioning yourself to receive God's gift of a new beginning. You can now rebuild your life, cautiously selecting friends, allowing only positive, healthy people in your life that will support you in your recovery journey. I know, with God's help, you *can* overcome this disease. I hope and pray you stay the course and continue your lifelong journey of recovery, taking one day at a time.

You have a beautiful and bright future ahead...

Your new life is filled with many exciting possibilities.

God is guiding you, and He will never leave your side.

It will be a challenging journey at times.

The pathway to recovery is narrow, with twists and turns along the way.

But God will never give you more than you can handle, with His help. Ask.

You will never be alone.

Many others will walk alongside you and will serve as guides along the way.

Your new life ahead can be rich with beautiful relationships and experiences.

The door is wide open for you to walk through.

The choice is entirely yours.

It's a matter of life or death.

Please, **never** turn back.

I love you, forever.

Mom

Ben Miller (photo credit: Rhonda Miller April 8, 2015)

Rhonda's last Mother's Day with Ben in Scranton, Pennsylvania
(photo credit: Rhonda Miller, May 8, 2016)

"We all make mistakes, have struggles, and even regret things in our past. But you are not your mistakes, you are not your struggles, and you are here now with the power to shape your day and your future."

Steve Maraboli

CHAPTER FIFTEEN

WE CONTINUE TO RECOVER

By John Shinholser
as told to Casey J.

I HAVE BEEN in recovery for the last forty years, and I want to share my message of hope. I always thought I was a bad person, but I was just a sick person who needed to get well. Addiction is a fatal, incurable, and progressive disease. But the key is to chase recovery, not drugs. Recovery is possible. 100 percent of the people I speak with regret relapsing; 100 percent don't regret recovery.

Putting it bluntly, I had a fucked up childhood. I was damaged goods by the time I was ten years old. I grew up with seven siblings. My daddy was a blackout drunk and very unpredictable. One day he loved us; the next day he beat us. My mama sent me to Catholic school and church, so I knew right from wrong. But what I was raised with and what I was living in were two different situations. I wanted so badly to escape reality.

When I turned eleven years old, I started drinking alcohol—a couple of beers here and there. I would get a little *whoopsie daisy*. It was fun. By the time I was twelve, I was a steady smoker and a steady sneaker of alcohol. By thirteen, I tried to drink whenever I could. At fourteen, I started smoking weed. At fifteen, I started experimenting with hallucinogens (LSD and shrooms). By sixteen, I was getting fucked up every day. I loved it. People always warned me to stay away from drugs and alcohol. Those people didn't know what they were talking about, because getting high was awesome. My primary concern was, *How am I gonna get more drugs?*

When I was fifteen years old, I started working as a painter. I made a lot of money. If I got paid on a Friday, I was broke by Monday. I couldn't go more than forty-eight hours without blowing it on drugs and alcohol. By the time I was twenty-one years old, I was borderline homeless in Denver, Colorado.

On January 16, 1980, I was recruited into the Marines and started boot camp two days later. I went from getting high every day to nothing. It was a huge adjustment and a big mistake. All I kept thinking about was, *How in the world am I gonna get out of this*? I seriously contemplated jumping off a ledge to break my leg so I could leave. I didn't though.

Shortly after my thought of jumping off a ledge, I was told that if I extended my contract for a year, I could choose any job I wanted on the list they provided for me. I scanned the list until I stumbled upon Field Radio Operator in Hawaii. Sign me up.

After three months of boot camp, I received three months of pay. I decided to go to downtown San Diego before leaving for Hawaii. I drank a few beers and ended up in a cheap motel room, full of passed-out Marines and strange women we had picked up along the way. I was broke once again and stinking of urine.

I packed my bags and went to Hawaii. Nothing changed. I couldn't stop getting into trouble. I got hit with five Article 15s (misdemeanors). The fifth one could have easily been bumped up to a court-martial, but it wasn't. I remember the colonel said, "Marine, you have two options: go to the brig or go to treatment." In the brig, I knew the food sucked and the women were fake, so I went to rehab.

Rehab saved my life when I was twenty-three years old. I had a guardian angel watching over me. I did forty-two days as an inpatient in the barracks. The rehab was run by people in recovery, and the counselors were really good. They made me get a sponsor and go to meetings; this is when I was introduced to the 12-step program.

I realized many things in treatment. I always believed that getting high was the solution to all my problems. In reality, all my problems stemmed from getting high. I had been arrested twelve times (eight times within the USA and four times in foreign countries) and each time it was because I was high—DUI, reckless driving, fighting, etc. Getting high was no longer the answer. I was forced to tackle my problems head-on and sober.

I was three or four weeks clean at the time, and I remember listening to this old guy talking about all the possibilities available once I completed the program. I wanted what these people had. So, with the help of my sponsor, I did the steps, and I did them right. I took charge of my life—the life I thought I had ruined. I surrounded myself with like-minded individuals who took recovery seriously. And when I hit that fifth step, it felt as if a weight had been lifted off my shoulders. I experienced my spiritual awakening and was finally set free.

Step work isn't a life sentence. If you do them and do them right, I guarantee you'll feel good about yourself. You'll gain self-respect. If you choose to do active addiction-related stuff you're going to get active addiction-related results, and the same applies to recovery. If you want to do well, you can do it.

Despite what many others may think or say, addicts are not dumb people. Addicts are smart and clever. If we want to do something, you can bet your ass we're going to do it. I fought for a better outcome and lost my desire to get high. It was an amazing feeling—much better than my best day wasted.

Once I got out of the Marines, I went back to Richmond, Virginia, and picked up where I left off in the painting business. Within a few years, I was doing over $1 million worth of business. I had twenty-five painters and seven trucks. I bought houses and did recovery work and service. I loved giving back to the community that helped me get sober. During this time, I met and fell in love with my first wife, and before I knew it, we were welcoming our daughter into the world. Life was great.

I was thirteen years clean, and out of nowhere, my wife decided she no longer loved me and wanted a divorce. I was blindsided and in disbelief. My heart was broken. I cried for two weeks straight. My friends in recovery kept an eye on me and made sure I was okay. Shortly after this time, I filed for bankruptcy. Despite all the negativity around me, not once did the thought of using cross my mind. I was determined to see it through no matter what.

Eventually, God was gracious enough to send me a real gem of a woman. I met her a year earlier at a convention, and then when I ran into her again, she was relapsing. Fortunately, she got help and recovered. I'm happy to say, we've been married for twenty-four years, and she's been clean for twenty-five years.

In 2004, my wife and I founded the McShin Foundation in Richmond, Virginia. (In 2022, Richmond was rated the number six city in the country for recovery.) Over the years, we transformed our 56-square-foot office into a 15,000-square-foot recovery center. We have 145 beds spread out among fifteen recovery houses. We are full-time providers of recovery support services in three different jails in Virginia. We have a multi-million dollar-a-year budget, and we offer a twenty-eight-day program. The McShin model is mirrored by many RCOs (Recovery Community Organizations) nationwide. We aim to help addicts get clean, stay clean, and become productive members of society.

Treatment is where people discover they need recovery. McShin is a triage center for newcomers wanting to get clean (and sober). We want them off drugs completely. People need to choose whether they want to continue getting high or recover. Over 60% of addicts are still in recovery a few years later. They know if they relapse, they need to get their asses back into treatment. Our foundation offers the resources they need to get well and hopefully stay well. Recovery is a life-long journey lived a day at a time.

The McShin Foundation has its jail programs as well. Over twenty years ago, I visited a jail that kept inmates who wanted to recover in the same unit and separated from the rest of the facility. This was exactly what I was searching for. I wanted to get other jails involved in following a similar system.

I was allowed to collect data on our programs, so one woman wrote her Ph.D. dissertation on them. She discovered that we reduced recidivism (a convicted person repeating the same crime) by 19% in one particular jail. We saved Richmond, Virginia, taxpayers $8 million in three years. In Pamunkey regional jail, 56% will recidivate after two years with no program. If you go through our program only 31% recidivate. This was proof that prison programs are effective (https://mcshin.org/about-us/data/).

I enjoy speaking at prisons. The inmates love when someone comes to talk to them. My presentations motivate them to consider recovery when they are released. I've visited jails in forty-four different states, and I would have hit fifty by now if COVID didn't fuck it up. I plan on fulfilling my bucket list by hitting all fifty states. I've even presented at prisons in England and Wales. It is my goal to spread my mission far and wide to help others.

Most people who have struggles want to be anybody but themselves.

When I look in the mirror, I'm okay with myself. I'm not bragging, I'm just saying, I'm proud of myself. I've had financial failures and successes. I'll be sixty-five years old in September, and I'm not concerned about my future. I don't fear death. I feel good about where I've been, who I am, and what I've become.

In the last nineteen years, McShin has helped 7,000 alumni. Unfortunately, 10% of those people are now dead from overdoses. Fentanyl is a real game-changer. Almost everything on the street is laced with it, causing the death rate to skyrocket over the last few years. Drug addicts who normally wouldn't have overdosed, end up dying from fentanyl poisoning. Just don't touch or buy anything off the streets. It's not safe. If you're thinking about using, please seek treatment before it's too late.

If you suffer from substance use disorder, you need to remember that the disease is bigger and more powerful than you. You need to accept the fact you are mentally ill. It is your responsibility to not use and to chase your recovery. You need to be the difference. You just need to take that first step. I promise you it will be worth it.

John Shinholser, co-founder of the McShin Foundation (photo credit: John Shinholser, 2022)

"The only person you are destined to become is the person you decide to be."

Ralph Waldo Emerson

CHAPTER SIXTEEN
WHY?

By Gracie Parker

HAVE YOU EVER wondered what it's like to have no mother, or no father in your life as a child? Never knowing your mom? Every time I see one of my friends or classmates with their mom or dad, it stings, it reminds me that I don't have a mom, that I never got to know my mom!

My name is Gracie Parker and I'm nine years old. That's been my life every day as long as I can remember. I am a child who lives with and is being raised by my grandparents. I often ask myself, why, why me out of all the kids? Didn't my parents love me? Why did they chose doing drugs over taking care of me and loving me? Why didn't they reach out for help, get help? Why can't I be normal, have a life with my parents? It's just not fair.

What could I have changed or could I have done to have the life I wish I had with my mom and dad? The answer is nothing because I was only six months old then and didn't know what was going on around me.

You see, my parents both did drugs, and they didn't have a job when I was born. My mom died when I was six months old, she fell off a seventy-five-foot dam and crushed all the bones in her body. She was found two days later. If you search "Woman's body pulled out of river at fall" on Google, it's on there. At the end of the article, they said "We will run toxicology tests." Nothing's updated, what happened? Was it an accident? Or something else? No one ever found out what really happened to my mom.

All I know is that I miss my mom so badly. What was she like? What did she enjoy doing? Looking at a picture I have of my mom, I have been told that I look a lot like her. That I have her hair. She never got to brush my hair, listen to me when I get home from school, comfort me when I am sad or hurt, take me shopping at the mall, or just pick me up from school. There are so many things we never got to do together. Why mom? I miss you so much! I wish you were here right now to comfort me as I am crying writing the story of my young life.

On top of all that, when I was little, my dad was hardly in my life, even though my grandparents tried to keep our relationship up whenever possible. One minute he was around then he was gone for weeks, months, or even longer. We have only spent one Christmas together a few years ago, and he slept through the whole Christmas Day. He might as well not have been there at all.

During a few times in my life, he would sometimes ask me if I needed anything or wanted anything, like one time I really wanted rollerblades, he said he would get them for me but never did. I ended up saving my birthday money and bought them myself. I always get my hopes up, that things would change, be different, followed by him disappearing and letting me down again and again. If my dad had a list of priorities, I feel like I am not on his list. I know I will never be the main character in my dad's life.

So, I may have a dad, but he isn't really a dad, he's only an acquaintance to me, a stranger in my life. When I talk with him on the phone or see him when he's not in jail or doing drugs, we have nothing to talk about, nothing in common, you know? A very big part of me feels dead. I should be worrying about getting my knee fixed if I fall, not what is going to happen next? Where is my dad, is he okay? Why doesn't he want to be in my life? What is wrong with me? I do love my dad ... but I am also angry, mad, and hurt ... it just hurts so much to be and feel alone.

I've always asked questions about my parents, like why am I living with my Oma and Opa? Why don't I have normal parents like other kids? For as long as I can remember speaking, my grandparents tried to answer all my questions, telling me what I wanted to know, and what they knew I could handle for my age. I was pulled out of a dangerous situation by my grandparents when I was just six months old. It could possibly be life or death for me to continue living with my parents. My life was in extreme danger. The house I was living in with my mom and dad before I was with my grandparents, was not safe AT ALL. Drug dealers, sex offenders, and criminals all roamed through the house at all times of the night and day when I was a baby. Calling my grandparents mom or dad, grandpa or grandma never felt right. So I have always called them Oma and Opa,

German for grandma and grandpa. My grandparents took emergency custody of me before my mom died.

On February 5, 2014, my Oma and Opa got permanent custody. For two years, my Oma and Opa tried to help my dad get off drugs so he could be my dad and be in my life. He's been in court-ordered rehab at least four or five times, but always ended up back on drugs and in the streets or back in jail. On May 16, 2016, I was officially adopted by my Oma and Opa. My dad gave up all his parental rights from jail.

That's my story. It's all really complicated, especially for a child. I deal with so many questions in my head every day. I don't know how I don't constantly end up in tears. When I see families together at the playground or at the store, I get anxiety attacks just thinking how I will never have that. I do so much volunteer work for and in the community, not for good looks but because I want to help out. I hope and wish that this will help me stay focused and take those thoughts off my mind. I have been volunteering at small events around town and have initiated several fundraisers, especially for the unsheltered! I started speaking at events around five years old, at small events like The Night Of Hope.

When I started to speak at that young age, I really only said little things like, "I lost my mom at six months old, and I don't see my dad." To be so young, I knew so much. Which in my case, for a child so young, it was sad because I knew what drugs were and that they are bad for you and that they can kill!

In September 2022, I spoke in Washington, D.C. at the Capitol at the "Trail of Truth" in front of 4,000 people. There were 1,200 tombstones that loved ones had made for their lost loved ones, whether it was a friend who lost a friend, a mom who lost a child, or a child who lost a parent. Unfortunately, I was one of many children who had a parent's tombstone there.

I often sit in my room, and stare at the painting my mom made for me, or I look at her picture. I always hope that this will somehow bring me closer to her. This painting and a baby book she started is all that I have of her. My Oma and Opa are always there for me, yet I need my trauma counselor to talk to as well. She had me tested and the result was that I have PTSD and minor depression. We are working on how to learn better ways for me to deal with this stuff, setting goals, and I get to see her every week. I thank God and my grandparents that I have her in my life.

Honestly, my feelings are so mixed I don't even know them anymore. I haven't had a mother, and I never will, is what I tell myself every day. You know, I would give the world to see my mother again. I have had dreams about dying, and then I would finally get to meet my mom and be held in her arms. When I wake up, I am anxious and depressed, but I also know that is not the answer for me. I can't do that, so pictures of her is all I've got. I have a half-brother, who I hadn't seen in seven years because we were separated after my mom died. We were finally reunited at the end of last year. To think about how many other kids are out there like me is sickening.

There are many reasons for children like me to need someone other than their parents, grandparents, etc., to talk to. WE ARE important, kids are told that they are seen not heard or not to say anything to anyone because of what people might say, etc. This is very wrong, and it is not right.

After talking with my friends and other kids, it is so clear to me that there is so much trauma that almost every child has to deal with, and many are on their own and have no one to talk to. Whether it's because of domestic violence, being in a foster home, with parents who are separated or divorced, or being bullied at home or at school. Maybe your mom or dad is in the military and got deployed; maybe a friend moved away or they have lost their pet; or worse, lost a loved one like an aunt or an uncle, brother or sister, or like me, their mom? Whatever the trauma, we need help!!! That is why I decided at the end of third grade to speak up and be a voice for children about what we are going through and what we need.

There is so much bullying toward orphans, fostered children, and adopted children, especially in the school system. I am hoping to raise awareness and keep on speaking up going forward because when parents and adults speak for us children, they don't know what our true feelings are. Parents and adults don't take into consideration that their child is hurting. We need someone other than our parents to talk to. It's super unfair, that our feelings are set aside, then we end up capsulizing it into a bottle and never talking about it again.

One part of my project is to get trauma counselors back into schools. You see, at the end of the 2021/2022 school year, the COVID funding for trauma counselors during COVID had ended at my school, but all funding will be gone by 2024 for all schools, from what I have heard. That was back at the end of third grade for me, and it made me so frustrated. I had trust with someone to talk to about my problems. Then, she was gone, trust was built then smashed into a million pieces. Thankfully, I still see her today because my grandparents take me to see her after school every week, but other kids like me aren't as fortunate.

2014 was the last time a Youth Health Risk Behavior assessment was done in my county that was anonymous. One of the items in the assessment showed that in 2014, 13% of middle school students had an actual plan in place to commit suicide. 13%!!! That is so crazy and scary to think about. We have lost nine years of data so far. We need this kind of data so we can get the help we need. These kids are hurting badly just like me. I am hoping to get trauma counselors back in school, especially at an elementary level.

I am hoping to speak many times at our school board and talk about this state and national, even international issue. I am setting up a group of kids like me, to talk about traumas and help them come up with ideas to speak or to see if they can support me. I have spoken to North Carolina state Senator Kevin Corbin, who is with me 100%. I hope to come back to Washington, D.C., with Truth Pharm in September 2023. Or even sooner to speak to senators, congressmen, and even the president. After I have accomplished my goal, I will NEVER stop speaking out about this issue because this issue will NEVER end. I am a victim with mental health problems and have experienced losing someone to drug use.

My voice will not be silenced. I WILL NOT BE A VICTIM WHO STANDS DOWN!

Gracie in front of her mother's makeshift tombstone at an awareness event in Washington, D.C., in September 2022 and the painting her mother created for her (2013). (photos credit: Gracie Parker and Elke Kennedy)

"The best way out is always through."

Robert Frost

CHAPTER SEVENTEEN

WHAT THE HELL'S
AN OXY?

By Ed Bisch
as told to Casey J.

"DAD! EDDIE'S NOT breathing, and he's turning blue!" My daughter's voice quavered on the phone.

"Call 911!" I screamed and hung up.

I glanced over at my co-worker, told him I had to go, and bolted out of the work computer room.

I hopped in a cab from Center City to my home in the nearby Fishtown neighborhood of Philadelphia. I urged the driver to hurry as fast as possible, all the while praying my 18-year-old son was okay. We pulled up to my house, and I saw an ambulance sitting out front. I breathed a sigh of relief. *Thank You, God.* I jumped out of the cab and noticed two men sitting in the ambulance. A sinking feeling consumed me.

"Sorry, sir," one paramedic said.

"WHAT?! Don't tell me he's dead," I gasped, panicking.

"We're sorry, sir. There was nothing we could do."

I ran into my house and found my brother crying.

He looked at me and screamed, "Don't go upstairs!"

He held me back when I attempted to approach the stairwell.

"What happened?" I sobbed in disbelief and shock.

"I don't know, but he's gone."

Within ten minutes, some of Eddie's friends appeared in front of my house. I hurried outside to question them.

"Tell me! Tell me! What did he do?" I pleaded.

"He did an oxy," one friend responded.

"An oxy? What the hell's an oxy?"

"OxyContin. It's like a strong Percocet."

"No, no. My son's dead in his bed!"

I went back inside and sat down at the kitchen table. I laid my head in my hands and sobbed. Just then, the police sergeant came in through the front door.

"OxyContin—kids are dying left and right from this shit," he said.

I popped up in a rage. I couldn't believe it. A new drug, and I never even heard of it. *How could this possibly be? How could this have happened? I read the newspaper and watched the news every day. How was it that the first time I heard the word, OxyContin, my son was dead from it?*

I took to the internet and searched Yahoo for OxyContin—a powerful extended-release opioid manufactured by a company called Purdue Pharma. Articles about OxyContin deaths and addiction filled the screen from states like Kentucky, Maine, and West Virginia, but nothing from the Philadelphia area. I thought to myself, I have to warn the kids!

That night, I faxed high schools a one-page warning about OxyContin—Eddie's school was the first of many. The next day, we called a press conference and every TV station in the city covered it at the 26th District Police Station. I did newspaper interviews. I went on message boards. I made it my mission to warn everyone, especially kids, about the dangers of OxyContin.

Eddie died on Monday, February 19, 2001, and by that Sunday, I was on a morning talk show. Three people called the show's producer and volunteered their time to create a website for me. I chose the first caller, John. He built a one-page website and within a week www.oxykills.com was online. My sister, who was a nurse, helped write the description from a medical standpoint.

Soon enough, I started receiving emails from chronic pain patients, saying how well OxyContin worked for them, and how "the abusers" are hurting them from getting the drug they needed. Many of the emails were very similar. Some were even nasty, saying horrible things such as: "I'm glad your son died. He got what he deserved." I would fire back, explaining that I just wanted to warn kids not to use it as a party drug. They said that my website's name would get their drug taken away.

On the other end of the spectrum, I also received multiple emails per day from people telling me horror stories about how they were prescribed

OxyContin and were now addicted or how their loved ones passed away from the medication.

The website had been up for two or three weeks when a Purdue Pharma representative reached out. She told me OxyContin was great if taken as properly prescribed. It was a miracle drug. It was FDA-approved. She stressed the safety of the opioid. Our email exchanges were very cordial, but she consistently defended the drug when I brought up news articles. I explained all I wanted to do was warn people about the dangers of the drug if abused. Warning others helped me cope with my grief, but a part of me still couldn't understand how this had happened.

As the weeks passed, a couple of Eddie's friends decided to tell me the full story about what happened the day before Eddie died. One of Eddie's friends threw a party at his uncle's house on Sunday, February 18. The schools were closed that Monday for President's Day. Eddie and his friend took Xanax earlier in the day, and that night, they drank some alcohol and split a 40 mg OxyContin pill. Eddie may have done more, but I don't know—and will never know for sure.

I learned that Eddie and his friends had been experimenting with pills for a while. They would take Xanax and drink some alcohol. The summer before he passed, he and his friends were testing out this new drug, Oxy-Contin. Oxycodone, the active ingredient in OxyContin, contains the same compounds as heroin. Eddie and his friends were not aware of the chemical similarity; they just knew it made them feel good. It is essentially heroin in pill form. No need to worry about impurities or needles—just rub off the coating and chew the pill to get the same effect. Teenage logic also came into play. Eddie's one friend told me they usually did 40 mg each, but because they took Xanax earlier that day, they decided to play it safe and split a 40 mg OxyContin. Well, that irrational thinking landed his friend in the hospital and Eddie in a coffin.

As soon as I learned that Xanax and alcohol played a role in his death, I updated the website to make it publicly known. Despite mixing drugs and alcohol (which I now know is called polypharmacy), I still believe OxyContin was the straw that broke the camel's back. My son would still be here if it wasn't for OxyContin. It wasn't long before a detective informed me that they knew where the OxyContin pills were coming from and were preparing to arrest a doctor—Richard Paolino.

Doctor Richard Paolino had an office in Bensalem, Pennsylvania, which is just north of the city. Drug dealers gave him a couple of hundred bucks and, in return, he would write out prescriptions for whatever they desired. At that time, the hottest drug was OxyContin. Although, he also wrote out scripts for Xanax. He was under surveillance for nine months before his arrest, and all I kept thinking was, *How many hundreds of thousands of pills hit the streets in that time? What if they could have busted him months ago? Would this have happened? Would my son still have died?* These thoughts wouldn't bring Eddie back, so I continued to focus on my goal. I was on a mission to save other kids in his memory.

In August 2001, Jim Greenwood (former U.S. Republican Congressman from Pennsylvania) presided over a hearing before the House Energy and Commerce subcommittee on OxyContin's use and abuse, in Bensalem, Pennsylvania, where Paolino was busted. I attended, not knowing what to expect. Purdue Pharma's Executive Vice President and Chief Operating Officer, Michael Friedman, Executive Vice President and General Counsel, Howard Udell, and Senior Physician, Paul D. Goldenheim, were in attendance.

Chairman Greenwood grilled them on OxyContin and the deaths associated with their medication. He revealed Purdue had access to IMS (Intercontinental Medical Statistics) data, so they knew how many prescriptions Dr. Paolino wrote. They knew exactly how many pills were flooding the streets. The Congressman demanded to know why they did not notify the authorities. Purdue's lawyer provided an answer that wasn't really an answer but legal mumbo jumbo. I left that hearing a little confused about why they didn't alert authorities. In time, their true colors would surface and the reasons would be revealed.

In 2002, I was part of the HEADSUP program with the Philadelphia police. We would speak at different schools, but I was allotted only five minutes to talk about pills. I wanted to start my program to focus on pills. Purdue offered to help sponsor a program where I would discuss prescription drug abuse. At this point, I still didn't fully understand what was going on, so I agreed.

I drove up to Purdue's headquarters in Stamford, Connecticut, where I met with Dr. J. David Haddox, Purdue's Medical Director. I told him that I was receiving a lot of emails from people who started as patients and were now addicted or from family members who lost loved ones to the medication. He stuck to the script and repeated the company line—"less than 1% of patients get addicted." He also reiterated the same emails I received from the chronic pain patients—that the addiction and death stories were preventing legitimate patients from obtaining the drug they needed.

I remember asking him if sales were down, and he responded, "Yes, by a lot." I left that day feeling a little uneasy, but I was also looking forward to starting my Prescription Drug Abuse Awareness and Prevention Program. Purdue even contributed a small donation to get the program up and running. I changed the website name from "OxyKills" to "OxyAbuseKills" to put an end to the harassing emails.

Three months after my visit, I almost fell off my chair when I read the headline in the paper. OxyContin sales were up 43% in the last year. BAM! It hit me like a ton of bricks. I realized my uneasy feeling was right. Purdue played me, just like they were playing the rest of the country. I rushed to my computer and shot off a few nasty emails to Purdue. I knew my website (which became a memorial for deceased loved ones) now required two missions—to warn people about the dangers of Oxy-Contin abuse and to expose Purdue's lies.

I soon learned that Purdue hired so-called pain advocates to troll the internet to repeat the company's lines. They also funded pain organizations that encouraged members to flood my website with similar emails. Furthermore, I learned that the "less than 1% of patients get addicted" line wasn't taken from a study, but from a short, five-sentence letter to the editor of the New England Journal of Medicine. It was a blatant misrepresentation and false statement, which the letter's author later testified to.

In 2003, I found a picture online of three moms protesting outside of Purdue Pharma's headquarters, with posters of their dead children, and felt compelled to connect with them. I contacted one via email. Soon, I was tipped off about Purdue hosting a lavish sales seminar in Orlando, Florida. We decided to protest. We called our group Relatives Against Purdue Pharma (RAPP). I flew down to another mom's house, Lee Nuss. I connected with her through my website after she lost her son, Randy, to OxyContin. We met up with around thirty other grieving relatives from California, Rhode Island, Georgia, and beyond. This was the second-ever protest against Purdue Pharma and OxyContin.

It was raining that day, and we were standing outside the entrance to the Caribe Royale Orlando. Parents and relatives were there, holding posters of their dead loved ones. A hotel maintenance worker came out, and said, "Sorry, I have to do this." *Do what?* Suddenly, she turned on a switch for the sprinklers, further soaking the already wet protesting RAPP members. The stunt backfired though, as a picture of us getting doused by the sprinklers appeared in multiple papers, along with a story about why we were there. We wanted accountability for the lives lost. We demanded the truth about OxyContin.

OxyContin was originally promoted for severe cancer pain; it was approved for moderate to severe pain. How was such a powerful drug approved for moderate pain? Well, it helps when you have someone on the inside to make it happen. Say hello to the FDA's Medical Review Officer, Doctor Curtis Wright IV (who a year after leaving the FDA was hired by Purdue at almost triple his FDA salary). In 1995, Purdue officials met with Wright for three days in a hotel room to draft up the application for OxyContin to guarantee its approval for moderate pain, along with the magic words that timed-release opioids were believed to be less prone to abuse. Never mind the fact that there were zero studies to back up this claim. Allowing this unproven wording was a golden ticket for the sales department and would change medical history.

Soon Purdue was pushing OxyContin for moderate non-cancer pain such as backaches, headaches, menstrual cramps, and even dental pain. OxyContin was launched in 1996 and by 2000, annual sales surpassed $1 billion—far exceeding the company's original projections.

If OxyContin was properly classified—for severe pain only—none of this would have happened. The FDA was complicit in igniting the opioid epidemic. RAPP attended FDA hearings to try to get OxyContin reclassified for severe pain only. A RAPP member, Barbara Van Rooyan, even went through the arduous process of filing a formal FDA petition to recall OxyContin until it was re-designed to be abuse-resistant and prescribed for severe pain only. We were surprised it was ignored for eight years and then denied. We felt we were going up against an evil empire, but we had to fight—too many were dying. We knew we were a team of Davids battling Goliath.

In 2003, RAPP attended the week-long trial in support of Karen White, a sales representative, fired by Purdue for lack of sales. Karen sued the company for wrongful termination. After seeing people with track marks on their arms during some office visits, Karen suspected possible pill mills. She refused to set foot in them anymore. She also refused to push 80 mg pills if a lower dose did the job. She had one lawyer. Purdue had ten on their team. Purdue needed to beat her to keep the records sealed. During the trial, the judge prohibited Karen from mentioning any of the deaths linked to OxyContin and would not allow other key evidence to be heard. Her lawyer was counting on a $2 million General Accountability Office (GAO) report, which detailed OxyContin abuse and deaths. Somehow, the Purdue lawyers convinced the judge to prohibit it as evidence, so they won even before the trial started. Purdue threatened to sue Karen for court costs, so she was forced to sign a nondisclosure agreement, sealing the records.

Justice did not prevail for Karen or for RAPP who just wanted the truth revealed. Years later, twelve of the thirteen medical professionals Karen refused to promote OxyContin to either went to prison or lost their medical licenses. Unfortunately, by that time, it was too late.

Around 2004 or 2005, I became aware of an investigation led by U.S. Attorney John L. Brownlee, in Abingdon, Virginia. The lead investigator, Assistant U.S. Attorney Rick Mountcastle, wrote a 120-page prosecution memo recommending criminal charges against Purdue Pharma executives. Rudy Giuliani and Mary Jo White lobbied for Purdue. The political appointees at the top of the Department of Justice sat on this memo, and the judge never saw it. Nineteen people, including ten RAPP members, gave victim statements at the sentencing. We begged for jail time. The judge was apologetic when he said he had to follow the guidelines.

In May 2007, Purdue Pharma's shell company, Purdue Frederick, only pled guilty to misbranding OxyContin and paid a record $600 million fine. The same three executives, who were at the first Congressional hearing in 2001, were fined $34.5 million and ordered to do community service. It was such a travesty. They deserved to be locked up, and all they received was the equivalent of a speeding ticket. The Department of Justice could have curtailed the opioid epidemic right then and there, but instead, it mushroomed into today's fentanyl epidemic. The people behind hiding this prosecution memo have the blood of hundreds of thousands on their hands. One day they will have to answer to a higher power for the carnage this settlement caused.

After the disappointing 2007 settlement, Purdue didn't slow down, and the FDA did not reclassify OxyContin. Instead, Purdue expanded its sales force, and sales climbed to $3 billion annually. As their sales grew, so did the devastating death toll. They continued to sell as much as possible and promoted the drug for thirteen more years. Purdue lied to everybody. They even lied to their own sales representatives. They claimed that if patients looked addicted, it was only pseudo-addiction. They weren't really addicted; doctors just needed to increase the dosage. You may wonder who concocted this fable, which was based on a single cancer patient—none other than the medical director who lied to my face, J. David Haddox.

Purdue was too rich and powerful. They put millions of dollars into PR and misinformation campaigns. They had every court case record sealed. Every time we thought we had them cornered, their money saved them. By 2012, I was burned out and frustrated. I decided to take a much-needed break. In doing so, my website fell by the wayside.

In 2018, the Massachusetts Attorney General, Maura Healey, sued Purdue Pharma and named members of the Sackler family who owned it in the suit. Soon, others followed and by September 2019, there were over 2,600 lawsuits against them, forcing Purdue to file for bankruptcy (which is ongoing and under appeal).

People are waking up to the corruption. Beth Macy's, *Dopesick: Dealers, Doctors, and the Drug Company that Addicted America,* the nonfiction book that later became an award-winning Hulu series; Patrick Radden Keefe's book, *Empire of Pain;* and Alex Gibney's HBO documentary, *The Crime of the Century,* expose the opioid epidemic in depth. People can watch these shows or read the books to learn more about the current opioid crisis in our nation.

Besides accountability, I believe we need what I call the 3Rs—supply Reduction, demand Reduction, and harm Reduction. All three are needed to slow the supply and slow the deaths and keep people alive until they're willing to get help.

Over one million people have died from drugs since OxyContin was launched in 1996, and until executives face real justice, these tragic stories will continue to pile up and repeat. RAPP held a rally, on December 3, 2021, outside the Department of Justice in Washington, D.C., demanding justice for the lives lost. Everyone knows someone affected by this epidemic. We will continue to fight for criminal charges against these professional drug pushers. If it wasn't for our efforts, the epidemic would be even worse. I couldn't save Eddie, but I know I helped save countless others.

Even after twenty-two years, I still have good days and bad days. I think about how great a chef Eddie would have been if he went to culinary school like he was supposed to. Now and then, I'll look at this picture I have of Eddie and his little sister when they dressed up as Batman and Catwoman for Halloween, and think, *How did this happen?* There are so many what if's and why's. So many regrets. But I know I did the best I could at the time.

Fighting Purdue Pharma and meeting so many other parents going through the same thing was my therapy, but you never get over the loss of a child. It changes you forever. You must learn how to live with it. The grief becomes a part of you. You accept it and move forward. I am thankful for all the wonderful memories I shared with Eddie—our fishing trips will always remain at the top of my list, especially the time Eddie caught a 36-inch striper on a charter boat at the seashore. It was a great day—a day I will cherish for the rest of my life.

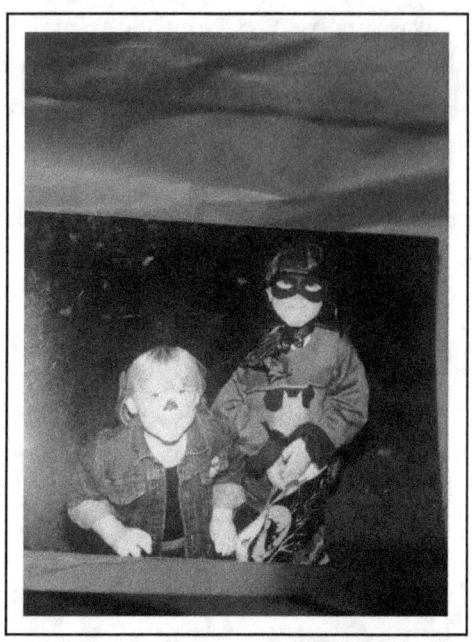

Eddie and his younger sister dressed up for Halloween, and Ed with Eddie catching stripers.
(photos credit: Ed Bisch, 1988 and 1999)

SPECIAL

ACKNOWLEDGEMENTS

W E WOULD LIKE to thank everybody who participated in our project and helped make our book come to life. Without all of you, this wouldn't have been possible. Thank you.

"I want to say thank you so much to my Oma (Elke Kennedy) and Opa (James A. Parker) for their love and support and for always being there for me. I love you both so much! And I want to say thank you to my best friend, "K-dawg," for always cheering me up." —Gracie Parker.

Thank you to our dedicated writers: Hannah Souders, Casey J., Nanci Hummer, Marigold Lombardo, Lynda Wallis, Isabelle Vargas, Ryan McLaughlin, Rhonda Miller, and Gracie Parker.

Thank you to our inspiring interviewees: Sherry Cooper, Officer Sam Hooper, Captain John Mazzeo, Al Bassetti, Toni, Lisa, Marly Gaviria, Tony Campolo, John Shinholser, and Ed Bisch.

Thank you to Coach Blu Robinson for writing such a powerful foreword.

Thank you to our trusted and knowledgeable editor: Brenda Lange (https://brendalange.com/).

Thank you to our helpful beta readers: Stephanie Muni, Alexa Bigelow, Marisa Foerter, and Leanne Subick.

Thank you to our thoughtful and sincere testimonials written by Danny Strong, Wesley C. Davidson, Joyce Hinnefeld, Charlotte Bismuth, and Michele Maize.

Thank you to our helpful indie publishing consultant: Mary (Stormy) Shafer (www.MaryShafer.com).

Thank you to our talented book cover designer: Gregory Del Deo.

Thank you to Phillip Gessert for formatting our manuscript into a real book and eBook (www.gessertbooks.com).

RESOURCES

WHY US KIDS

Founder Gracie Parker
North Carolina
www.whyuskids.org
Whyuskidso@gmail.com

SPEAK UP FOR BEN, INC.

We support families who have experienced the stigmatized loss of a loved one from a substance-related cause or a family member's addiction, to come out of the darkness of the isolation of grief and into the light of a safe community to heal. Based in Bethlehem, Pennsylvania, our nonprofit operates the OASIS Community Center to provide family support in a gathering place for families to heal, learn, and grow.

Rhonda Miller, CFRS, Certified Grief Educator
Co-Founder | Executive Director

www.speakupforben.org

OASIS Community Center
Nurturing Families Impacted by Substance Use

We offer educational programs, therapist-led groups, peer support groups, and wellness activities. All programs are free of charge. Everyone is welcome.

Rhonda Miller, CFRS, Certified Grief Educator
Founder | Executive Director

484-747-6825
www.OasisBethlehem.org

SAMHSA (Substance Abuse and Mental Health Services Administration)

National Helpline 1-800-662-4357
https://www.samhsa.gov/find-help/national-helpline

DEA

United States Drug Enforcement Agency
Recovery Resources
https://www.dea.gov/recovery-resources

The McShin Foundation Richmond, Virginia

1-804-249-1845
https://mcshin.org/

TaKE Center, L.L.C. Outpatient Rehabilitative Services and Equine Assisted Therapy Program in Kintnersville, Pennsylvania

https://www.takecenter.com/
terrillklong@gmail.com | Phone: 610-730-5115

Anthony Campolo, LPC, LCADC, DBTC, CCTP, ACS

https://www.campolocounseling.com/

Ryan Elizabeth McLaughlin

Licensed Acupuncturist and Chinese Medicine practitioner
Flourish of Life Medicine
www.flourishoflifemedicine.com

Relatives Against Purdue Pharma (RAPP)

https://www.facebook.com/RAPPedB/
@EJB1893

Addict II Athlete

Coach Blu Robinson, CMHC, SUDC
Head Coach of Addict II Athlete
Clinical Mental Health Therapist, Substance Use Disorder Counselor
https://www.addicttoathlete.com/

Please feel free to reach out to our writers at
shatteredauthors@gmail.com

"Believe you can, and you're halfway there."

Theodore Roosevelt

www.ingramcontent.com/pod-product-compliance
Lightning Source LLC
Chambersburg PA
CBHW070706130626
46553CB00005B/1859